THE
WORKING
MOM'S
GUIDE TO
MANAGING
STRESS AND
THRIVING

THE WORKING MOM'S GUIDE TO MANAGING STRESS AND THRIVING

Jessica N. Turner

© 2018 by Jessica N. Turner

Published by Revell
a division of Baker Publishing Group
Grand Rapids, Michigan
www.revellbooks.com

Spire edition published 2023
ISBN 978-0-8007-4487-8 (mass market)
ISBN 978-1-4934-4249-2 (ebook)

Previously published in 2018 as *Stretched Too Thin: How Working Moms Can Lose the Guilt, Work Smarter, and Thrive*

Printed in the United States of America

Some content in chapters 2 and 4 is adapted from *The Fringe Hours: Making Time for You* by Jessica N. Turner (Revell, 2015).

Unless otherwise indicated, Scripture quotations are from THE HOLY BIBLE, NEW INTERNATIONAL VERSION®, NIV® Copyright © 1973, 1978, 1984, 2011 by Biblica, Inc.® Used by permission. All rights reserved worldwide.

Scripture quotations labeled NLT are from the Holy Bible, New Living Translation, copyright © 1996, 2004, 2015 by Tyndale House Foundation. Used by permission of Tyndale House Publishers, Inc., Carol Stream, Illinois 60188. All rights reserved.

Published in association with literary agent Jenni L. Burke of D.C. Jacobson & Associates, an Author Management Company, www.dcjacobson.com.

Baker Publishing Group publications use paper produced from sustainable forestry practices and post-consumer waste whenever possible.

23   24   25   26   27   28   29   7   6   5   4   3   2   1

Author Note

Dear reader,

I'm coming out of a season of being stretched too thin as I write this to you. My publisher has given me multiple extensions on this short letter, yet I am still writing it at the very last minute. I'm exhausted. I've been working too much, eating poorly, and taxed as a parent. I don't sound like a good teacher for this book, do I? Stay with me . . .

I share this update because if you are reading this book, you can probably relate. I want you to know that we are not that different. However, the one thing that might be different is that you likely feel stretched too thin often, whereas I can clearly see that this period is temporary (and is now ending, thank goodness). This is a huge and notable difference. We are not meant to live stretched too thin, despite the hustle culture we see idolized in the media and in many books. So if that is where you are, your life is about to change, thanks to this little book.

When I wrote this book six years ago, my life looked really different. I was married and worked in corporate America. My children were all in day care and elementary school. Since that time, a few things have changed for me, including going through a very public divorce and leaving my corporate job to be a full-time entrepreneur. My life now includes raising teenagers, dating, and co-parenting with my ex-husband.

But even with all those changes, I am proud to say that the principles in this book still hold up. Inside these pages are tips and tools that are doable and accessible for a busy woman like you. If you read this book with an openness to evaluate your own life, you can pivot to positively impact every aspect of life. It isn't going to be easy. It might mean you have to start saying "no" more. But every "no" is a "yes" to something else—hopefully to you and your loved ones.

The cliché is true—you can't pour from an empty cup. My hope as you read this book is that you discover or rediscover what has been missing in your story. You can go from feeling stretched too thin to thriving. You have already taken the first step by opening this book. I believe in you.

Cheers,
Jessica

To my mom, Debbie LoCoco,
one of the hardest-working women I know. I love you.

In memory of my grandmothers,
Marilyn LoCoco and Ruth Schim. Thank
you for always believing in me.

Contents

Introduction

One Saturday in mid-September, my younger son, Ezra, and my daughter, Adeline, were playing with building blocks together on the circle rug in our living room. This rug sits in front of a bay window and some bookshelves and is where the kids spend many hours playing with their toys. A few Cheerios were sprinkled on the rug, spilled from breakfast a few hours earlier, and the washing machine was churning in the nearby hall closet. I was sitting on the couch, responding to a few work emails and catching up from being out of the office the Friday before. As I glanced over at them playing, I took a breath and smiled, not wanting to forget the beauty and simplicity of the moment.

To outsiders looking in, the scene would have appeared to be an ordinary one in the home of a very regular family. And they would have been right. But to me, I saw something more.

My kids . . . playing and happy.

Chores . . . getting done.

A few moments free . . . to do what I needed to do.

That scene captured, in part, what thriving looks like in my own life. Your scene likely looks different, but the feeling is the same.

You know the feeling I'm referring to—the one when everything (or almost everything) feels right in your world. You feel at peace. You feel happy. You feel alive.

A few weeks later, with Halloween around the corner, I called my husband, Matthew, on my lunch break to talk about the forthcoming weekend. On deck was a postseason soccer party for my eldest son, Elias, and book writing for me (I had ten days until my deadline). I also really wanted to go to the pumpkin patch, but doing so was going to be difficult because the farm was only open on Saturdays from 10 to 5 and Sundays from 1 to 5. Our littlest napped during the afternoon, and the soccer party was going to run during most of the pre-naptime prime hours. As we wrestled with our options, I started to cry.

Yes, I was crying over wanting to go to the pumpkin patch.

For me, the pumpkin patch represented family (something we could all do together), the kickoff to fall and Halloween (one of my favorite times of the year), and tradition (we go every year). Because of my work schedule, I had already missed many traditions and activities, and that realization left me weeping on the phone with my husband while sitting in the parking lot of Panera. In response to my breakdown, my husband gently and patiently assured, "We can make this work, honey." And he was right. We did. I wrote early in the morning. Then we went to the pumpkin patch and the party, my toddler got his nap, and I completed my work. I even had time to craft in the evening.

These two examples reflect the yin and yang of being a working mom. Some weeks we have flexibility, and all seems right with the world. Other weeks we are crying from stress, overwhelm, and "missing out."

As working moms, we are constantly making choices about how and in what to invest our time. The more we can do that's not rooted in guilt and comparison but is instead an output of joy and love, the better life is.

Working motherhood is not easy, but it has taught me a great deal. When I take time to practice intentionality, really listen to my family members, take care of myself, and love the work I do, I find myself thriving. Sure, dishes may be left on the counter and the laundry baskets may never be empty, but that's okay. I have systems in place to ensure we never run out of diapers and toilet paper, and eventually, all the projects get completed—even if the timeline isn't always what I'd like it to be.

Thriving as a working mom involves knowing who you are and loving the people closest to you well. And that's what I want you to find too.

I believe work and motherhood can coexist in a positive, invigorating manner. Yet for too many women, that's not the case. For the past eighteen months, I've explored what it means to be a working mom by talking with moms all over the country to learn what brings them joy and their struggles. The resounding refrain I heard over and over again was this: *I'm stretched too thin.* If that sounds like your story, this book is going to help you make positive changes. I want working moms to be able to say with pride, "I love my family. I do great work. I'm thriving."

This book is a permission slip to reprioritize yourself, make changes to your day-to-day life, and embrace a new normal that is free of feeling stretched too thin. In the following chapters, I will unpack the greatest struggles we working moms have, including boundaries with our work; fostering meaningful relationships with our spouses, kids, and friends; practicing self-care; and managing our homes. Frankly, every one of these topics could be a book! But in the space available, I'll offer insights specifically geared toward the working-mom experience that will equip you to do life a bit differently.

The mission is to help you recognize that contentment can be cultivated amid the busyness of life. Happiness and joy are yours for the taking every single day. Yes, living this way takes intention, dedication, and drive. But you already have all of that. Each of us was born with an innate desire to live well.

I know you will be inspired by the wisdom shared in the following pages from working moms across America who are just like you. Their stories and insights will motivate you to become the woman you yearn to be.

Remember as you read that the journey toward thriving is just that—a journey. It can be messy and complicated. But that doesn't mean you can't still prosper and be joyful.

I love how my friend Jyl, who runs a successful network of social media influencers, puts it: "Don't be afraid to fail forward. I believe one of the biggest keys to happiness is growth. The more we grow and reach our potential (which means trying, falling, but failing forward so we grow), the more we increase our resiliency, our strength, and improve our talents. All of this increases our happiness, because we are progressing, reaching our true potential, and moving forward. As we do this, we will be an example to our kids and everyone will be happier."[1]

Struggle, guilt, and failure are part of the journey, but these experiences are not the destination and should not define your life's story. You can be a working mom who isn't overwhelmed by her to-do list or constantly feeling as if she is failing at everything. You can and should be able to see the value in the work you do, appreciate your unique contributions to your family's life, and look at life with positivity.

This book isn't the answer to everything—or even to most of the things. But it is a guide to help you stop feeling stretched too thin. That doesn't have to be your norm. So let's bounce back, find our rhythm, and cultivate a thriving life of contentment.

ONE

Evaluating Your Present

Do you ever wonder how you survived certain seasons of life because they were so busy that you could hardly breathe? Maybe you are in one of those seasons right now. A few years ago, I lived that way for an entire year. And while I lived to tell about it, I never want to be stretched that thin again.

In 2015, in the span of twelve months, I delivered my third healthy child, released two books, blogged for multiple big brands, and engaged with tens of thousands of people who followed me on social media. I also worked a full-time, nine-to-five job. In the same year, my husband signed a children's book deal and traveled overseas with a major media company.

While much of it felt like a dream (New baby! Book releases! Overseas travel!), the year was also incredibly taxing. I was exhausted, burned-out, crabby, and not really living life but merely surviving. I would say to myself, *Just get through today, this week, this month, next month*—but there was no end in sight. Our house was a mess. I was yelling at our kids. And I hated myself.

I was crazy busy and stretched too thin.

One Sunday evening that November we had some friends over for dinner and to watch *The Walking Dead*. After they left, I was in the

15

kitchen, scraping leftover Pioneer Woman potato soup into some CorningWare, when my husband, Matthew, half teasing/half serious, suggested, "Why don't you start lunches while you're in here?"

I snapped back a bit too quickly, "No, I have work to do."

He sighed. "When are you not working? You never stop. You are missing out on your kids."

"Don't say that," I replied.

"Why not? Someone has to say it to you."

"Soon," I said. "Soon, I won't have so much work." I was, after all, releasing that second book, and the holiday season was a busy time for my blog. But that voice inside my head told me I was just making excuses. I was always busy. I knew Matthew was right.

While I wanted to assure myself that things were going to be different soon, I knew things would not really change because I always found or created more work. For me to have less work, I needed to draw that proverbial line in the sand and fully commit to doing less.

A month later, on New Year's Eve, I wrote these words across the top of a goal-setting journal: SLOW DOWN. That was what I wanted for the next year and for the rest of my life.

That didn't mean I was going to sit around and do nothing. It simply meant I was going to evaluate how I was spending my time. Writing that phrase was my proclamation that I would seek out a more intentional life.

My perspective has shifted a great deal since that crazy year. While my life is still busy, I am not working at the same breakneck speed. And instead of being stretched too thin, I am content and satisfied with my life. But getting here took some intentionality.

Examining Your Present

The journey to thriving as a working mom must begin with an honest look at your present circumstances and the pressures that threaten to or already have overwhelmed you. Where are you feeling stretched to the breaking point?

We live in an era of speed. The norm has become to get things done faster, to move faster, to go faster. Our society has normalized nonstop activity. Because of this busyness, we often feel we don't have the room to make intentional choices about how we spend our time or to live true to ourselves. Instead of living well, we are living stretched too thin.

I know that my can't-breathe-because-I'm-too-busy experience a few years ago is one that is relatable to other working moms because, during the summer of 2016, I surveyed two thousand of them, asking one question: What is your biggest struggle as a working mom?[1] As you might imagine, the answers I received were vulnerable, honest, and, when read between the lines, often filled with pain, emotion, or exhaustion.

Here is a sampling of what these working moms, from all walks of life and professions, had to say:

> The hardest thing I struggle with is being stretched too thin and finding time just for myself in the midst of parenting, being a good spouse, and nurturing that relationship.

> I'm stretched too thin, so I feel like I'm not being the best mother, wife, friend, daughter, and business owner. I feel as though trying to make time for everything is impossible. It is difficult to give 100 percent to any one thing.

> Since becoming a mom four and a half years ago, I've struggled with losing my identity. While I love being a mom, I gave up all my hobbies in pursuit of balancing work and family life. My marriage seems to be an afterthought. I haven't worked out consistently in years. Overall, I'm stretched too thin, but I cram in as much as I can in the four hours a day I see my kids awake. It's depressing to lose your identity, lose your body, have every relationship changed (marriage, friends, parents, co-workers), and it is not something anyone can prepare you for.

> Lately, I feel like I've been stretched too thin in all areas of life and that there truly is no balance. If I try to give more attention

to one area, another area suffers, and I feel like all the areas need my full attention, which can be quite stressful. I also feel like I give so much of myself at work that I'm tapped out by the time I'm at home and need to give my kids attention. Even though I have a supportive husband who does help out around the house, many of the home management tasks, especially cooking and keeping up with appointments, still fall to me, and I often feel like I'm working two full-time jobs! The area that I neglect the most is definitely self-care, and when I do try to make a diligent effort to include it, it often feels like one more "task" in my already busy schedule, which adds to my stress.

What stood out to you in those statements? As I read those heartfelt responses, I couldn't help but notice all the ways women expressed being *stretched too thin*. The phrase was like a drumbeat. Work. Kids. Activities. Church. The list of reasons women felt this way went on and on. It was also clear that many of these women had stopped taking care of themselves in the midst of their busyness, finding it impossible to make the time. Can you relate?

Living stretched too thin is the norm for many working mothers, but it doesn't have to be. We truly can live with purpose, experience love, and be content with both a family and a career. Throughout this book, we are going to look at the areas in which working moms frequently feel overwhelmed and discuss practical ways to make things better. You are going to find many ideas in this book. As you read, remember that not everything is going to be applicable to you at this time. Moreover, it is impossible to implement *all* the ideas and strategies you'll find here. Give yourself permission to be choosy, and read with an eye for what will work in *your* life during *this* season. Avoiding being stretched too thin is not about overhauling everything. Instead, it's about recognizing what changes you can make to help you thrive on a day-to-day basis, then making conscious choices to make those changes a reality.

Taking Inventory

Before changes can happen, it is important to take inventory of your present in a very eyes-wide-open manner. No one else's story is exactly like yours. So to make the principles in this book apply to your life, your input is vital.

What does life look like for you right now? Are there things on your schedule that you dread every day, every week, and/or every month? The working mother experience includes some unique challenges related to responsibilities, parenting, and practicing self-care. You need to own both the good and the bad, not sugarcoating any of it. At the end of each chapter, you will find questions to consider and journal about. For this process to be effective, you will want to be detailed in your inventory. Think of the major areas of your life, such as parenting, work, marriage, and self-care, and really evaluate your investment in each and how much time you spend on them. Don't skim past this important work.

You might be thinking, *I know my life. I know what's in it, and writing things down isn't going to be helpful.* But seeing all the things written down in one place is incredibly eye-opening. By having a clear understanding of your present, you can effectively change your future.

Begin your inventory of the present by looking at the mental load you're carrying as a working mom.

Understand Your Mental Load

For many working moms with young children, summer brings a whole new set of challenges to manage—many dealing with what to do with the kids. If your job doesn't allow for a lot of flexibility, summer camp can be a great option. My kids love camp, and I have learned to embrace their summer schedule instead of feeling guilty for not spending endless days at the pool with them. That said, summer camp planning is a burdensome task that begins months in advance.

Where I live, many of the best summer camps fill up in February and March, which means I need to start planning right after Christmas. Yes, it's as crazy as it sounds. I remember the first year when I had to schedule camps for two of my three kids. I spent lunch breaks at work researching camps, using a blank calendar printout to pencil in schedules and plan. Cobbling together camps that my art-loving daughter and outdoor-loving son would like was a challenge, but I managed to find a few that I could enroll them both in. This was a huge win because one camp meant for much simpler drop-offs and pickups.

One of the camps both kids wanted to enroll in opened registration at 10:00 a.m. on a Saturday in February. This camp typically sold out right away, so I made sure to have our profiles filled out in advance and set an alarm on my phone.

As luck would have it, our toddler woke up sick the morning of camp registration. My husband had an appointment that Saturday, so I found myself with all three kids at the pediatrician's office for a 9:15 a.m. appointment. This was not how I had planned our Saturday, but I did what anyone would do—I brought my laptop with me to the appointment. Our doctor diagnosed an ear infection and confirmed the pharmacy she would send the antibiotics to. I then said thank you and asked if I could stay in the examination room for a few minutes to submit a camp registration. She laughed, remembering the days when she was doing the same for her kids.

Sick kids.

Busy schedules.

Medicine.

Summer camp registration in February.

Just a typical day of managing all the things! Tell me you can relate. You see, many working moms are also their home's manager. In my case, registering for summer camp was one of the many items on my to-do list for that Saturday. You could likely replace summer camps with a dozen other examples of your own. Mothers tend to be the ones who oversee household tasks, delineating what needs to be done by whom, etc. Sometimes family members become so used to this norm that they are dependent on receiving direction from the mother. Moreover, she is then forced to carry the bulk of the household's mental load.

This "mental load" that a person carries is defined by work-life balance coach Marie Levey-Pabst as the "largely invisible work of remembering and noticing."[2] Because this load is carried inside our heads and isn't visible in the same way going to an office is, we often don't recognize it as real work. We lump it in as "what moms do," mentally reducing its significance and burden.

When I first heard this term—mental load—I wanted to jump up and down because, finally, the story of my life has a name! So, what is your mental load? Some examples might include the following:

- awareness of your children's health and wellness (Did they nap today? When is their next physical? Are they still seated next to the bully at school?)
- managing family and friend relationships (scheduling get-togethers, attending athletic events, etc.)
- noticing household tasks that need to be done (burned-out lightbulbs that need to be changed, chores, maintenance projects, etc.)
- planning meals for the week, and creating grocery lists
- taking care of your family's finances (paying bills, managing bank accounts, etc.)
- researching and planning family vacations and special events (ordering tickets, booking flights, etc.)
- shopping for birthdays and holidays
- recognizing when your children's clothes are too small, when it is time to reorganize and shop for seasons, etc.

Carrying a heavy mental load is exhausting. Marie notes, "While everyone has a mental load, women carry a disproportionately high amount of the mental load in a family."[3] And when you add work to the mix, you have a working mother whose mind is always in overdrive.

Recognizing what is a part of your mental load and determining how to release some of its weight is critical to feeling less stretched too thin. Some of these things you should let go of, while others you can and should delegate to others. I'm fortunate that my husband is always willing to pitch in and help. I find that I simply need to ask, particularly when I am feeling unequally yoked with home tasks.

Identify Your Core Values

Also important to understanding your present is identifying what you value, because living in a way that aligns with your values is a choice. Living stretched too thin often means you are running on autopilot, going from one thing to the next. You aren't mindful of the things you are investing in. Taking time to identify your core values can help you shift where you are putting your energy.

What is a core value? A core value is something that is deeply important to you. It spans your roles as professional, wife, mother, friend, and person.

The way we live showcases what we value. If you are a person who values friendship, you will be a person who invests in others. If you are a person who values family, you will spend quality time with those you love.

Do you know what your values are? Can you name them?

For most women who are feeling stretched too thin, that feeling comes as a result of busyness in their lives. If that is true for you, do you value busyness? My guess is probably not, despite the fact that your life may reflect otherwise. Recognizing that busyness is a value you are showcasing is the first step to shifting your mentality and taking steps to live a life that reflects what you truly value.

Separate the Need-to-Do from the Nice-to-Do

My guess is that, since you are reading this book, you feel the tension of juggling many roles and responsibilities and desperately wanting to do everything well. Unfortunately, to-do lists are often overwhelming, and there is only one you. Is it any wonder that life tends to feel as if you're always running on a hamster wheel? I don't know about you, but I've often stared at the various things I've put on my calendar and wondered, *How is it possible to do it all?*

The answer? It's not. We have twenty-four hours in a day and one life to live well. That said, I believe you can live a full, even busy, life without the cycle of busyness controlling you. I know this sounds impossible, but stick with me. If you intentionally choose and control the busyness you accept in your life, that busyness is not a burden like the busyness that overtakes your life and controls you instead. Wholeness, peace, and happiness come when you are living with intention.

You need to regularly evaluate the need-to-dos versus the nice-to-dos to ensure you are living fulfilled. If your life is cluttered by unnecessary things, trimming the fat, so to speak, can have wildly positive repercussions.

To do this, your perspective needs to change from doing *all* the things to doing only the things *that really matter*. This subtle shift takes time and practice, but it changes everything for the better.

Prepare for the Unexpected

Sometimes we are living stretched too thin, with days heavily booked and deadlines looming, and then the unexpected happens. An illness. A death. A major household expense that we didn't expect. A school project that is due tomorrow that was forgotten. Whatever the cause, the result is a tailspin of additional stress and shifting of priorities.

I have had more than my fair share of these situations, and they often happen during my busiest seasons. The worst experience happened last year when I was traveling for work and had an unexpected health scare. For several days, I pushed through the pain, thinking that Advil and some other over-the-counter medications would help me get over it. Eventually, the pain was too great, and I had to cut my trip short and book an early flight home. My husband immediately took me to the ER, and twelve hours later, I was in surgery. The recovery took weeks, and it hit right during a season when I was already stretched too thin. I remember crying and asking, *Why is this happening right now?* I needed to work. I was supposed to host a baby shower that weekend that would have to be canceled. And I was concerned about the financial strain of the health-care bills.

My nurse gently reminded me that during the healing process, I could not immediately jump back into things at one hundred miles an hour. I needed to slowly build up my strength and give myself grace. This unexpected slowdown was a reminder that many things that cause us to be stretched too thin should not rule our lives in the way that they do. If something takes more time to complete than we originally planned, we will still be okay.

The busyness of everyday life doesn't always allow for flexibility, but if we can work toward not scheduling our time without breathing room and allowing for more space in our days, these unexpected hurdles will be less overwhelming.

My friend Sara passed away a few years ago. As someone with a debilitating disease that forced her to be homebound, she knew better than anyone the challenges life can bring. She once wrote in a daily devotional, "I want you to be fully awake to the blessings in your life and not miss a moment. Take them in and savor them in your senses as if you might lose them tomorrow."[4] We should remember her reminder to live fully awake when we feel overwhelmed by the unexpected.

Reflections on Your Present

What Is Your Present?

To move from living stretched too thin to thriving, you must first understand your present. Running on autopilot is no way to live. You must assess your mental load and recognize its burden. You need to be able to clearly articulate your core values so you can make choices that reflect those values. Living with a value-based perspective allows you to say no to nice-to-do things and yes to need-to-do things. Take time using the questions that follow to assess your present, with the knowledge that what you write could change your life.

What is your current job? _____

How many hours do you work each week? _____

How happy are you with your job? _____

On the next page is a grid containing areas in which working moms commonly feel stretched. Make notes about each area as it relates to your own life and any tensions that are present. For example, in the marriage/relationship box, you might write, "My husband and I both work full time. We have two small children, and after they go to bed, we are both tired and want time to individually catch up on our favorite TV shows, projects, etc. Consequently, we aren't getting the quality time we need."

Work	
Children	
Marriage/ Relationship	
Home	
Friendships	
Self-care	
Activities (i.e., church, school, community)	

Does your life have other areas of tension that need to be addressed? If so, please note them below. _____

_____

_____

_____

_____

When you think about your mental load, what is a burden to you? _____

_____

_____

_____

Do you think your priorities are in order, or have they gotten out of whack? Why? _____

_____

_____

_____

_____

What are your core values?

_____

_____

_____

_____

In what ways are you investing in those values? In what ways are you spending time that doesn't relate to your values?

_____

_____

_____

_____

What's one change you can make to live in a way that better reflects what you truly value?

_____

_____

_____

_____

TWO

Setting Yourself Up
for Success

One summer my to-do list was a mile long, and I was stretched too thin in every aspect of my life. My kids had a lot of needs, I had several big deadlines looming at work, I was working on some new projects for my online business, and my house was a wreck. I was overwhelmed, and all I could do was cry as I pushed through each day. At one point, while sobbing to my husband, I said, "I just want to get to Sunday so I can relax." In that particular moment, surviving the week felt like the only goal I could achieve.

Have you been there? Maybe you're there right now—feeling like if you can just get to the end of the day, the week, the month, things will somehow be better, get better. When you are stretched too thin, you may have difficulty finding clarity. You attend to whatever needs your attention at the moment. You do not have the energy or the space to do anything more than complete the task at hand and go to the next thing. Your life feels like a pinball machine in which you are the ball. Months go by, and when you look back, you don't know what you did or how you really spent your days, only that you have bounced from one thing to another.

If you want to achieve radical change in your circumstances, setting goals is an effective way to start. The task of goal setting might feel overwhelming, particularly if you are currently stretched too thin. I get that. But making it a priority will serve you well in the long run.

Why Set Goals?

Before we begin, let's consider the advantages of setting goals. As you read through the following benefits, think about how setting goals could transform your own circumstances.

- *More time.* When you set goals, you give yourself permission to spend time on things that truly matter to you. You also begin to say no to the things that are distractions from what you want to accomplish, thereby giving you more time. It is amazing how much time we spend on things we don't want to do! Goals can help eliminate these time sucks.
- *Increased clarity.* When you are living stretched too thin, you have little clarity. You are like a robot, moving from one task or appointment to the next. Setting meaningful goals gives you a lens through which to make good choices for your life. Suddenly, things that are not tied to your goals become easier to let go.
- *Eliminated procrastination.* You often know what you need to do, but because you have not set goals, you put off doing the work to get there. Setting goals ensures that you stop procrastinating and start taking action.
- *Increased motivation.* Goal setting is inherently motivational. Determining your goals will energize you to achieve them.

- *Positive energy.* Having goals that are purposeful is invigorating. When you are working toward your goals, you will be inspired and have a more positive perspective.
- *Increased control.* When you work toward a goal, you find you are more in control of the actions you take in life. This is a very rewarding feeling, particularly for someone who has been living stretched too thin.
- *Improved life satisfaction.* Overall, when you are working to achieve goals that are important to you, you will be more satisfied.

I hope this list energizes you. The goal-setting exercise you're about to undertake has the power to impact numerous areas of your life.

Goal-Setting Exercise

In the past, I struggled with designating the time necessary to go through the goal-setting process. I always found more "important" ways to use my time. But that perspective was shortsighted. Designating the time to set goals means that something else can't get done. True. But here's the thing: every yes means a no to something else. Say yes to this investment because the long-term benefits outweigh the short-term loss of productivity in another area.

Step 1: Consider Your Past

The practice of thoughtful goal setting begins with preparation. When you think about goal setting, your thought process is probably future focused. That makes sense, since goals are all about where you want to go. But before you can cast a vision for the future, you need to remember where you came from.

Remember the scene in *The Lion King* in which Rafiki and Simba are talking about the past and Rafiki hits Simba on the head? Rafiki then goes to do it again, and Simba ducks. Rafiki delightedly cheers, saying you can either run from the past or learn from it.

Your past is a great teacher. It reminds you of the best and the worst moments of your life, and it allows you to grow, learn, and appreciate those experiences. When you look at your past, you can more easily cast a vision for what you want for your life moving forward.

As you look back, think about the positive experiences and the struggles, particularly as they relate to your life as a working mom. Start with the positives and be specific. Ask yourself questions such as:

- What things have I done well in my journey as a working mom?
- What am I proud of?
- What are my strengths?

Then consider the struggles. Again, be specific. Ask yourself questions such as:

- In what areas have I encountered struggles?
- What felt overwhelming?
- What are my regrets?
- What changes would I make if I could?

For both lists, consider the lessons you learned. Seeing how experiences have helped you grow is an important step in the goal-setting process. Doing so enables you to see clearly how the actions you take impact your life.

The good, the hard, and the downright bad all blend together to enrich your story and to ensure that the goals you set for the future are appropriate and right for your life. As you review your past, don't be afraid to ask your spouse, close friends, or co-workers for their insights. They will likely provide a different perspective that will bring value to your goal-setting experience.

Step 2: Brainstorm Goal Ideas

Lara Casey, working mom of three and creator of the Power-sheets goal-setting journal, encourages goal setters to brainstorm a list of ideas. The act of jotting down a bunch of ideas will help you refine the few goals you want to pursue. Once you have written them, Lara advises, "Check your goal ideas to make sure they are rooted in what matters. It's easy to make goals that sound good, or goals that other people have that you think you should have, too, just to keep up. Don't do that. How you spend your time is how you spend your life. Check each of your goal ideas to see if it's worth spending your time on."[1]

For your own goal setting, as it relates to cultivating contentment in your life, focus on what you evaluated in the previous chapter about your present and what you would like to change. Identifying the challenges you would like to overcome will motivate you to create inspiring goals.

Step 3: Write Intentional Goals

Now that you have reflected on your past and brainstormed a list of ideas, it is time to focus on writing goals that will transform the way you work, parent, and do life in general. Intentional goal setting can have a profoundly positive impact on all these areas in both the short and the long term. Being purpose driven in your goals—in both the practical and the visionary—will help you live your life with deeper intention.

One of the country's most popular goal-setting methods is the SMART system (specific, measurable, achievable, realistic, and time-bound). After attending a goal-setting seminar with Michael Hyatt, I adopted his SMARTER system, which I think does an even better job of helping people write achievable goals. Here is a summary of the seven keys to Hyatt's SMARTER system:

1. **Specific.** Goals should be very specific. General goals aren't as easily achieved because they lack detail. So be as specific as you can with your goals, and write them in a fashion that defines the result you want to attain.

2. **Measurable.** Make sure the results you're seeking are quantifiable. If you can't measure a goal, you won't know when you've succeeded.

3. **Actionable.** Set active rather than passive goals. Your goals should start with an action verb. Talk about what you will do rather than what you will be.

4. **Risky.** Push yourself outside your comfort zone. Goals that are risky are more compelling, and they're more likely to be achieved.

5. **Time-keyed.** Goals should have a deadline. Open-ended goals are too easy to put off for another day.

6. **Exciting.** Make sure your goals are personally compelling for you. When a goal excites you, you will be motivated to work on it. Consider what will give you that fire in your belly.

7. **Relevant.** Your goals should be relevant to your current season of life and to your values.[2]

With these ideas in mind, edit your list down to two to three goals. Less is more if you want to successfully achieve your goals. By having a short list, you will be able to be hyper-focused on achieving your goals. People who set more than three goals are unlikely to achieve them.

If you have a goal that seems overwhelming, break it down into bite-sized pieces. For instance, when I commenced my work on this book, I set the goal of finishing it by the end of September. I used my contracted word count to figure out how many words I needed to write each week to achieve that goal. Each week I documented my word count on the calendar to motivate me to meet the deadline and achieve my goal of handing in my manuscript on time.

One additional tip I'll offer is this: write your goals with a positive tone, focused on the good that will come from achieving them. For instance, instead of writing, "Leave my crummy job," you might write, "Find a job in the next six months that leverages my strong people skills and gives me flexibility to work from home." Or if you are writing a goal about your home, instead of writing, "Organize my messy house," you might write, "In October, hire a professional organizer to help create organizational systems that will reduce clutter and create a happier and more peaceful environment for my family before the holidays."

Easy enough, right? Okay, maybe writing goals won't come easily at first, but I've found this system to be incredibly helpful in writing motivating, achievable goals. Goals are not about making you feel inadequate. Instead, they are about helping you be intentional to get to where you want to go. When written thoughtfully using the SMARTER system, goals can help you find relief from the push and pull of daily life.

Step 4: Pursue Your Goals

After you have drafted your goals, hang them someplace where you can review them every day. This visibility will ensure that your goals remain a source of inspiration and motivation. Some people make a goal a password on their computer. That way they type it every day. I adopted this idea and found that it helped me to keep my goal front and center in my mind. The password served as a continuous reminder of what I wanted to accomplish, and I made a point to consider what I could do to make the goal a reality every time I typed that password. Once I hit the goal, I changed my password.

I used to find setting goals difficult because I had seen myself fail again and again. I would see only the gap between my goal and what I had actually achieved. Once I turned my thinking on its head and focused on the strides I had made, I was able to see the value in the goal-setting process.

If you feel discouraged about a goal or want to quit, step back and think about why you set the goal in the first place. What is it that you want to achieve? What will happen when you meet that goal? In the case of finishing this book, completion resulted in being paid my remaining advance (always a good thing!), encouraging other working moms, speaking opportunities, and more. These rewards were incredibly motivating, particularly in moments when I didn't want to sit at my computer.

Considering your own rewards for a goal can be beneficial during moments of frustration throughout the process.

Tracking Your Time

In addition to setting goals, you need to have a clear sense of how you are currently spending your time. Chances are you could highlight the big things you are doing with your time fairly easily. But the minutiae (like how much time you spend doing laundry each week) might be a little harder to pinpoint. Gaining perspective on where your time is going will help you determine what is working and what changes you could and should make in your daily and weekly habits to ensure that you achieve your goals and live with contentment.

That is why I want you to track your time for a week. Tracking your time involves recording everything you do over the course of a day every day for seven days. Think of it as similar to keeping a food journal or tracking the steps you take in a day. Write down everything you do—school carpool, meetings, errands, laundry—in fifteen-minute increments. After you track your time for a week, ask yourself the following questions (space for answering these questions is available at the end of this chapter):

- Where did I spend my time?
- What items are nonnegotiables (e.g., work, taking kids to school, etc.)?
- What time was wasted?
- What activities could be streamlined in my schedule? (For instance, does doing laundry every day make sense, or would it be better to do it as a marathon on one day?)
- Am I doing too much? Do I need to be better at saying no?
- Did I do anything just because it would have made me feel guilty to not do it?
- Would it be helpful to ask for or hire help for any of the things I spent time on during the week?
- Did I take time for myself? If so, how much time?
- Overall, how did I feel this week? Happy? Tired? Stressed? All of the above? How did these emotions impact me and my activities?

The act of tracking your time and then carefully evaluating it is an eye-opening experience. Every time I track my time, I am reminded how effective documenting my life in this fashion can be. Seeing all of my activities, not just my workday, as a whole noted on one document gives a lot of perspective.

Use the insights and information gathered to make needed changes to your daily and weekly habits. For instance, you might recognize for the first time that you are spending an average of five hours a week commuting to and from work. Seeing this amount of time might motivate you, as it did me, to alter your commuting habits.

A few years ago, I made the decision to use my commute time to invest in me rather than just mindlessly listen to the radio or chat on the phone. I began listening to audiobooks in the car, which became an incredibly life-giving habit. At the end of the year, I realized that this new habit had enabled me to listen to at least a dozen books that year. And because listening to audiobooks makes me happy, I was happier both when I got to work each morning and when I got home each night.

I was first introduced to time tracking by Laura Vanderkam, one of the nation's experts in how we spend our time. Laura has evaluated hundreds of time logs, and over and over again her research has shown that when people track their time, they see that they do have free time. More importantly, though, time tracking nudges people to reevaluate how they use their time. I expect this will be true for you too, so please, do this important exercise. I promise it will be well worth it.[3]

These two activities—setting goals and tracking your time—will enable you to make life-changing alterations to how you are living your life. Meaningful change cannot happen unless you first know where you are and then determine where you want to go. Do not be afraid to do this important work.

Reflections on Your Goals and Time

What motivated you to read this book?

Think about and record three goals for where you would like to be in ninety days. Think bite-sized and attainable yet risky goals. Follow the SMARTER system. Writing down these goals, even if they seem small right now, is like drawing a line in the sand. Putting pen to paper is a powerful first step in creating change in your life.

For example:

Goal 1: Establish a routine that includes one hour of exercise three times a week.

Goal 2: Do not respond to work email in off hours.

Goal 3: Read to my children every day.

Your turn:

Goal 1: _____

Goal 2: _____

Goal 3: _____

Now make a copy of those goals and hang them somewhere visible. For extra motivation, make one of the goals a password you regularly type.

One of the best ways to get a sense of what life looks like right now is to track your time during a continuous seven-day time period. (See appendix for a time-tracking chart.) Use the time-tracking grid to record everything you do in one week. At the end of the week, review the way you spent your time. Add up the hours you spent on major tasks such as work, kids' activities, home management, etc. Then answer the following questions:

Where did I spend my time?

_____

_____

_____

What items are nonnegotiables (e.g., work, taking kids to school, etc.)?

_____

_____

_____

What time was wasted?

_____

_____

_____

What activities could be streamlined in my schedule? (For instance, does doing laundry every day make sense, or would it be better to do it as a marathon on one day?)

_____

_____

Am I doing too much? Do I need to be better at saying no?

Did I do anything just because it would have made me feel guilty to not do it?

Would it be helpful to ask for or hire help for any of the things I spent time on during the week?

Did I take time for myself? If so, how much time? _____

_____

_____

_____

Overall, how did I feel this week? Happy? Tired? Stressed?
All of the above? How did these emotions impact me and my
activities? _____

_____

_____

_____

THREE

Discovering the Feelings Within

t was the end of the school year, and my five-year-old daughter, Adeline, came home with a bulging red folder of worksheets and projects she had done during her first year of kindergarten. One was a stapled "book" recapping her school year. Every page contained her kindergarten letters spelling out her school, friends, and memories, complete with crayon illustrations. You know the kind—stick figures with disproportionate heads and no noses.

As I flipped through the packet, smiling and taking it all in, I saw a grid titled "My Four Memories from the Year." In the lower left quadrant was "Daddy," with a drawing of Adeline and her daddy in her classroom.

Rather than seeing it for what it was—a precious drawing by a little girl who loved having her daddy come to her class—all I saw was that Mommy wasn't in the picture. Adeline's simple crayon stick-figure artwork triggered all the mom guilt, all the struggles of being a working mom. It was the proverbial straw that broke the camel's back. I looked at the picture and immediately started bawling, with big crocodile tears pouring down my cheeks.

My husband was astonished at my outburst. "Why are you crying?"

"Because she is going to remember *you* being at school and *me* in an office," came my quick reply.

Adeline was right there when all this happened, and my reaction made her respond. She put her small dimpled hand on my arm, and as she gently rubbed it, she said, "Mama, I'm sorry. I forgot when you came to the Valentine's party and we took pictures." I brushed my tears aside and told her not to be sorry and that I didn't mean to cry. I hugged her tight and tried to compose myself.

After Adeline left the room, Matthew and I talked about how I was feeling. He reminded me that I *am* a good mom who is there for our kids all the time and that they will remember that I loved them deeply and was present in their lives while also working hard and having a successful career.

Our talk made me feel better in the moment. But the truth is that as I am writing these words, I'm tearing up. Because that working mom guilt is a real thing. And no matter how hard we fight against it, it rears its ugly head now and again.

In this chapter, we will evaluate some of the key emotions working moms have difficulty dealing with as well as explore some practical advice for managing those emotions. Now, this doesn't mean those emotions are always bad or that it isn't okay to feel them now and again. Instead, what I hope we will accomplish is learning how to recognize those feelings for what they are and address them in a healthy manner.

The Struggle Is Real

Our feelings greatly impact the way we see ourselves and how we interact with others. As I have spoken with working moms across the country, I have been overwhelmed by the vast emotions that play out in our lives, particularly when we are stretched too thin. The sheer volume of responsibilities coupled with the stress of accomplishing all we need to do results in emotions that feel uncontrollable. Licensed counselor Dawn Sturkey explains, "Women are processing emotionally and cognitively at the same time. We have more neuro connections between the two hemispheres of our brain than men do. We are constantly, constantly, constantly going. I can be totally engaged with a client and also know that it is the time my son is driving home from school because that is the way our brains work."[1] This dual processing sometimes makes us feel like we are in overdrive.

Bill and Pam Farrel wrote a popular book called *Men Are Like Waffles, Women Are Like Spaghetti*. In an article, they explained their spaghetti analogy this way:

> Women process life more like a plate of pasta. If you look at a plate of spaghetti, you notice that there are lots of individual noodles that all touch one another. If you attempt to follow one noodle around the plate, you would intersect a lot of other noodles, and you might even seamlessly switch to another noodle. That is how women face life. Every thought and issue is connected to every other thought and issue in some way. Life is much more of a process for women than it is for men.[2]

It's true, isn't it? We are like spaghetti, continuously touching multiple things at the same time. Because of the natural overlap that happens, it is easy for our feelings to get involved. This can then directly impact the way we navigate the tensions of work and motherhood.

Here is some of the feedback working moms in my survey offered when I asked about feelings they struggle with:

> Managing the guilt and unreasonable expectations that plague me even when my brain tells me I am doing great.

It is impossible to manage everything, and I constantly believe that I'm letting someone down. There is tremendous guilt in working outside of the home—but I bring home an important income for our family budget and my job carries the insurance for my family.

I feel like I'm crazy busy doing so many things, but I don't feel like I'm doing any of it good enough. I feel like I'm doing everything last-minute.

There's never enough time or energy! I'm exhausted when I finish work so that I don't feel I have anything left in the tank to "pay forward" to the rest of my life!

I feel like I can't do anything with excellence. I constantly feel like I'm shortchanging my kids when work is inflexible or demanding or that I'm shortchanging work when I have obligations or events for my kids. It's defeating.

With my schedule and the kids' schedule, I face a lot of guilt. Guilt that I don't spend enough time with my kids during their critical years. Guilt that I don't give enough attention and time to work to remain impactful. Guilt that I don't devote enough time to myself. Guilt that my spouse and I at times coexist to manage our crazy lives with kids. Finally, I struggle keeping up with day-to-day tasks (keeping up with the house).

When I'm at work, I'm thinking of home and my children, all that needs to be done and all I want to do. By the time I get home, I'm exhausted and feel like my energy has all been spent.

Did any of those statements resonate with you? I've seen myself in every one of them at one time or another in my life. At any given moment, a working mother's mind and heart can be overflowing with a variety of feelings—fear, joy, guilt, passion, worry, and more.

While some of those emotions are unavoidable, many of the feelings we experience are self-imposed.

For example, my children's school was having a cake walk for an annual fund-raising event, and though I was having a stressful week at work, I felt obligated to bake a cake to bring in. When I got to the sale, I noticed that the majority of the cakes surrounding my homemade cake were store-bought. That's when I realized that all the extra stress I had experienced had been my own fault. Rather than joining the other parents who had brought perfectly yummy cakes from the grocery store, I had allowed a bad case of mom guilt to add more stress and frustration to my day.

It's important to recognize the presence of these feelings and discover where the root cause is. In the instance of guilt driving me to baking that cake, this was because of my desire to be a "good mom" while feeling overwhelmed. I somehow equated baking with excellence in mothering. But that was a lie, an unnecessary pressure that had been created by me.

We all have examples of this in our parenting journey. Mom guilt, comparison, fear of missing out, and the struggle to feel satisfied are normal. But we can't let those feelings eat at us or become the standard by which we live because they will only cause us to feel small, unloved, unworthy, and disappointed. Living in the shadow of these emotions isn't fair to us or the ones we love.

Below is a list of the most common stressors and emotions cited by working moms in my survey. Next to each word, write your reaction to it. This could be a memory of a specific time you experienced that emotion, or it could just be how the word makes you feel in general. For instance, next to guilt, you might write, "I feel guilty for missing my child's sports tournaments because I have to work." Or next to overwhelmed, you might write, "I am overwhelmed when it comes to managing my home. I can't get on top of things." If a word doesn't resonate, cross it out and move on.

self-doubt	
guilt	
inadequacy	
comparison	
shame	
overwhelmed	
exhausted	
expectations	
responsibility	
judgment	
fear	

Now that you have considered each of those words, I want to share some good news with you. You are not alone. More importantly, none of your feelings define who you are. Do not let these feelings steal your joy, your capacity to be your best, or the essence of who you are. Working moms are phenomenally capable, loving, driven, passionate women. We are a blessing to our families, our friends, and our co-workers. Do not let your emotions undermine your self-worth and calling.

Righting the Emotional Ship

The goal of discussing these emotions isn't to say that all emotions are bad or illegitimate. Frankly, the opposite is true. Our feelings can often help us to recognize when something is not right in our lives, such as when boundaries have become relaxed, relationships have become strained, or priorities have become out of whack. In those instances, feelings can be helpful in motivating us to grow and make different choices in our lives.

That said, in other instances, we simply need a kick in the pants to right our minds and hearts. While the following advice isn't going to solve everything, it will hopefully help you to overcome the negative feelings that rise up and to approach life with a healthier perspective.

Become Self-Aware

Self-awareness is the first step to overcoming feelings of negativity. By recognizing their presence, we are better able to cope conducted change the way we react to those feelings. In an interview I conducted with licensed psychotherapist and mindfulness coach Iman Khan, she said, "I think true self-awareness comes from the ability to understand how to be the observer and not the participant in your experience."[3] She advises that to cultivate self-awareness, we need to learn to report on our experiences without attaching an interpretation, drawing conclusions, or predicting an outcome. Over time this reporting will enable us to quickly identify when we are reacting from a place of a hurtful emotion and to handle things differently.

"To continue to be self-aware, we have to be able to develop a unique curiosity of our lives, and just be curious without judgment," added Iman.[4] For example, the next time you feel guilty because you had to attend a work function instead of going to a child's basketball game, be curious about that sense of guilt. Recognize its presence and evaluate its root cause. You'll find that self-awareness will cause a shift in the way you handle situations.

In my own life, I find that summer is a particularly challenging season for me as a working mom. This past year I recognized how much I dealt with guilt about the fact that my kids were going from summer camp to summer camp while my husband and I worked. I also felt jealous toward the moms who were at the pool with their kids in the afternoon instead of in an office like I was. That self-awareness motivated me to change my perspective.

My kids and I made a summer bucket list. As I read over that list, I realized that the picture of "a perfect summer" I had created in my head did not align with my kids' ideas of a perfect summer. Their desires were simple: a family day at the zoo, a water balloon fight, a canoe ride on the river near our home. And those were all things we absolutely *could* do—even with me having a traditional day job. As a result of our summer planning, my summer turned from one riddled with guilt and jealousy to one full of joy and delight—all because I was aware of how I was feeling and made a change.

Give Yourself Permission

As trite as this may sound, give yourself permission to be you. You are not a robot without feelings. Life impacts you. Giving yourself permission to be your truest self, to pursue your career, and to miss things from time to time provides freedom from the shouldas, couldas, and wouldas.

While writing this book and working a full-time, nine-to-five job, I had to give myself permission to let some things go. I missed many of my kids' soccer games because I had a deadline. I leaned on my husband more to handle chores that I typically did. Ultimately, I stopped holding myself to unrealistic and unattainable expectations. If I hadn't, I would have easily become overwhelmed, unable to do my work or anything else.

Once you stop trying to be someone you are not and doing things that don't align with your desires and/or your responsibilities, you are better able to thrive in your life.

Stop Keeping Score

Too often as working moms we feel as if we are competing against someone or something and need to keep score of how we are doing. This needs to stop. The sooner we can break free from this habit, the sooner we will be more content with our circumstances.

For instance, I had three days until I had to turn in a project. My kids had their first soccer games that Saturday morning, and I planned to work that Saturday afternoon. However, my husband and son were gifted with tickets to an NFL game for that afternoon. My son had never been to a pro game before, and of course I wanted them to go. But I couldn't find a babysitter, so having Matthew gone for the afternoon meant I was going to have to squeeze three days of writing into two. My husband very rationally said to me, "There will be more soccer games. Just skip the games today." He was right. Though I felt a little mom guilt at first, by not keeping score with the other moms who would be at the soccer fields, I was both less stressed and a better mom because I got my work done.

Remember, nobody is keeping score, so do what you need to do—or not do.

Focus on What Matters to You

An easy way to get sidetracked and start living a life you don't want is by focusing on what other people are doing instead of what you want to do. For instance, I *love* throwing big birthday parties for my kids with handmade decorations, elaborate games, and amazing cakes. But I have had parents say to me that my parties make them feel inadequate, which breaks my heart. Throwing elaborate parties is *my* thing. If your thing is doing a small gathering with immediate family, awesome. Focus on what really matters to you and your family. Don't look left or right. Stay the course.

The same advice applies to your career. Don't look to what others are doing in your office or profession to gauge what you should be doing at the present moment. Instead, focus on what matters to you and what makes sense for your career. Psychotherapist Patti Sabla says that too often "we end up doing things out of obligation instead of out of interest."[5] By recognizing why you make the choices you do, you will be more thoughtful regarding what you invest your time in.

Have Hard Conversations

One of the easiest ways to stop negative feelings from festering is to have hard conversations. I recognize the irony in saying that a hard conversation is an easy fix. But once you swallow the pill and do that hard thing, you experience an immediate freedom. Career coach Bobbie Hurley advises that these hard conversations take practice.

> Most people avoid conflict, but sometimes you have to sit down, and you have to have that hard conversation. Whether it's a team member that's not working correctly, if it's a child that's just out of line, or if it's a spouse that's not helping out. It's hard to sit down and have that conflict. You worry about people being upset with you and what people think of you, but if you have those hard conversations, they get easier, and it's easier to stand up for yourself. So you have to do it repeatedly. It's not just a "I'm going to stand up for myself one time, and then I'm just going to be cured and have plenty of time to myself and not be stressed anymore."[6]

Because I work full-time, friends sometimes don't invite me out, assuming I will be too tired or going out would add too much to my day. After multiple instances of feeling left out, angry, and jealous, I finally confronted a friend about the way I was feeling. Doing so was hard because I knew she didn't mean to hurt me and I didn't want to come off as whiney or needy. I told her how not being invited made me feel and asked her to invite me and let *me* make the decision about whether I would attend instead of just assuming I couldn't. What started as a hard conversation ended with us crying and hugging—and with things getting so much better. If I had not had that conversation, not only would I have continued to feel bad, but the situation could also have become divisive, leading to the end of a friendship. Instead, being honest and having a hard discussion made us closer and helped to eliminate future hurts.

Recognize the Impact of Financial Stress

Many women work because it's financially necessary for their families. So financial concerns can place an additional layer of stress on many working moms. For some, the stress might come from making ends meet, while others might become overwhelmed if they don't feel fully equipped to weigh all of the complex financial decisions that can come with caring for a family.

If finances are a burden and cause significant stress in your life, consider finding a course, book, money-saving blog, podcast, or other education opportunity to help you gain confidence in making the right choices for your financial situation. A financial planner can also help give unbiased financial advice related to investments, tax laws, and insurance decisions.

We have experienced tight financial seasons in our family, and they were tough! I remember going to the Dollar Store to buy a single box of garbage bags because we didn't have enough money to buy the normal Glad box I liked from Target. I started reading coupon blogs like *Money Saving Mom*, *Passion for Savings*, and *All Things Target* to learn about shopping with coupons, leveraging sales, and living differently, and it made a huge difference with our finances—and our stress levels!

Forgive

Sometimes things happen to us, and we hold on to resentment and anger, refusing to forgive the person who hurt us. Unforgiveness is like a poison in our lives. It will eventually impact every relationship, every experience, every moment of life. I have seen it wreak havoc in a loved one's life, and it is heartbreaking, hurtful, and relentless.

If you have some forgiveness to give, I encourage you to do that mighty work. You see, the benefit of forgiveness is for you, not the other person. Do not let a circumstance define you and the way you live your life. Forgiveness brings freedom and wholeness. It doesn't erase what has happened to you, but it allows you to heal and move forward with grace and wholeness. Jen Hatmaker writes in her book *Of Mess and Moxie: Wrangling Delight Out of This Wild and Glorious Life*, "[Forgiveness] liberates us from the crushing responsibility to oversee the resolution, which may or may not ever come. It removes any authority another person holds over our wholeness. . . . Forgiveness clears the way for new growth. . . . We can still live."[7]

Stop with the FOMO

Fear of missing out (FOMO) is a real thing, particularly thanks to social media. Getting caught up in what others are doing and experiencing can be so easy, especially if you are working when something is happening.

For many working moms with young kids, mom groups can be the source of FOMO because they typically meet during the day. Kate Lehman, a social scientist at UCLA and working mom of two, found that texting other working-mom friends helped her overcome her FOMO related to those mom groups. She explained, "I text them about work and mom stuff and often have open-ended conversations going on with them. This helps a lot since I can feel connected to other mamas without having to show up on a Tuesday morning at 9:30."[8]

Pediatrician Jennifer McHugh-Barker, mom of three, shared her own FOMO experience:

I spent much of my children's younger years thinking I was miss-ing out on everything—hanging out on the playground with other moms, not having enough playdates for my kids, even girls' nights out. But after a while, I was exhausted and still feeling like I was missing out. At one point, I just decided it wasn't worth it. I would do the best that I can do, and while sometimes that may not seem enough, I cannot live my life worrying about "what if." . . . Ultimately, I think when you have three kids and you are working full-time, you just start to realize where you have to draw the line or you will lose your sanity![9]

If you sense feelings of FOMO rising inside you, simply force yourself to stop and see what you do have or are experiencing. Oftentimes a forced pause can be enough to abate those feelings. It's also helpful to remember that becoming consumed with what you might be missing out on does nothing for you or your family. Instead, it breeds negativity and resentment.

Turn Off Social Media

Social media can breed resentment, comparison, FOMO, and jealousy. So turn it off, unfollow people, or limit how much you use it. Do not let it distract you from the beautiful life you're living.

During a heavy work season, I found I was using social media frequently. It was like a window to the outside world because I was spending so much time at my office. Eventually, I noticed that I would click the Facebook app on my phone without even realizing it. So I deleted the app from my phone. Not having it there felt strange at first, but within a few days, I found I was more present in my life.

Working mom Tiffany Tucker made the drastic decision to completely remove social media from her life and said it was an awesome decision.

I mostly did it because I would get so worked up about the social and political things being discussed on social media. I've stopped looking at my news feed, and I have to say I am happier and more emotionally even, without the highs and lows that come out of nowhere when something pops up in my feed. Sometimes I don't know what's happening to someone I never talk to, but for my close friends, we hang out and talk and I know what's happening in their lives.[10]

If you don't feel the need to turn off social media, maybe consider if you should unfollow certain people. Over the years, I have learned that if a person's profile is causing me to feel inadequate, jealous, annoyed, or angry, I simply need to unfollow them. This act made me feel guilty at first, but now I recognize that it is healthy and good behavior. I can certainly still look at their profiles if I want to, but I do so on my own terms. Control your social media so it doesn't take control of your emotions.

Let It Go

Just like Elsa in *Frozen*, many times you just need to let things go. Good enough is the new perfect. You are not Wonder Woman, and you can't do everything. Be content with where you are and what you can accomplish. Some days—or weeks—you need to let the chores wait because of other commitments and responsibilities. That is okay. Recognize that you can only do so much and that sometimes you just need to let things go.

I know in my life I have had to let stacks stay stacked and laundry stay in baskets longer than I would have liked because of time constraints. And you know what? It was all still there when I could get to it. No long-term damage done.

Letting things go also relates to any feelings you might be holding on to that are preventing you from being your best self or living your best life. Hanging on to feelings like anger or resentment only hurts you. Unclench those fists and release those feelings.

Trade Comparison for Celebration

Instead of comparing your experiences to someone else's, celebrate their experiences and celebrate the blessings in your own life. Research shows that when we practice gratitude, it has a positive impact in every area of our lives. I can attest to that from my own experience. I am always happier when I am consciously celebrating the good things in my life. This also has a positive impact on how I parent my children. I want to leave them with a legacy of gratitude, and I can't do that if I am not living a grateful life myself.

Don't "Should" All over Yourself

A play on words, this popular sentiment emphasizes that using the word *should* in regard to habits and actions is not helpful. Career coach Tammy Gooler Loeb says, "The moment you hear the word *should* in your head or it comes out of your mouth, just know that's not serving you. You get to write the book of rules."[11]

Should is a word that can regularly creep into our heads. Here are a few examples shared by other working moms:

"I should clean my house more."

"I should take my child to this event."

"I should not bring so much work home."

"I should call my friends more."

"I should exercise."

"I should volunteer at church."

"I should be able to do it all."

Release yourself from the shoulds that might be holding your mind captive and controlling the choices you make.

Notice and Squash Your Inner Critic

You know that voice in your head that is always negative? Squash it. This type of negative self-talk is deceiving and destructive. Noticing when you start a critical dialogue in your head is the first step to eliminating it. Once you notice the dialogue, replace the words with more positive or accurate statements. Oftentimes your inner critic is black-and-white or speaks in broad brushstrokes. Instead of saying, "I am the worst mom ever," say, "Today wasn't my best day parenting, but I have had many other good days and will try to do better tomorrow."

Examining evidence that supports or refutes the statements you make about yourself can also be helpful. For example, the next time your inner critic calls you the worst mom ever, stop to really think about that statement and you'll quickly realize it's not true, thereby proving that your negative self-talk is inaccurate.

Practice Self-Acceptance

When you are stretched too thin, accepting yourself just as you are can be challenging. During seasons of overwhelm, I have found myself quicker to nitpick little things about myself, and I extend myself no grace. If this sounds familiar, try practicing self-acceptance. Recognize that the world has only one you, just as you are, today. You are uniquely made, and your gifts matter. Consider the things you do well, and recognize that no one's life is perfect. Show yourself the same love and compassion you extend to your family.

Determine Your Purpose

Take time to explore your unique gifts and to write a personal purpose or mission statement. Evaluate your successes, core values, and goals. Then draft a statement that articulates who you want to be as a person. This self-reflective exercise can be grounding if you feel pulled in many directions. When you determine your purpose, you can use it as a guide for making choices in your life and for eliminating things that fall outside the scope of how you want to live.

Consider sharing your purpose statement with someone close to you, such as your spouse or a dear friend. They can provide feedback, if you wish to receive it, and encourage you on your journey to fulfill your defined purpose.

These tactics aren't the fool-proof formula for never feeling emotions like stress, guilt, and jealousy. But when embraced, they can definitely make a positive impact on your outlook and daily perspective.

Being a working mom is tough, and you are not alone in the struggle to be happy while having a demanding life. Take some time today to look at the feelings that are most prevalent in your life, and consider these solutions. I hope that at least one will help you thrive as you move forward this week.

You Are Strong

Working mothers are some of the strongest women I know. They navigate so many responsibilities and roles in a given day and, for the most part, are quite successful in doing so. Read through the following list and write down a word or phrase that the word inspires about your own life.

accomplishment	
pride	
provision	
satisfaction	
love	
joy	

peace	
energy	
hope	
self-worth	

Did that exercise remind you of how awesome you are and what an incredible life you have? I hope it did. Seriously, think about everything you do in a given day. It's astonishing. Sometimes I blow my own mind thinking about everything I do *before I leave for work*—permission slips, laundry, lunches, tending to crying kids, writing, connecting with my husband, and more—all in the span of about three hours. Then I go to work and do a bunch more before going back home to do even more. The strength we need to manage so many tasks and handle the emotions that come with life is substantial, and we often don't give ourselves enough credit.

In Marcus Buckingham's book, *Find Your Strongest Life: What the Happiest and Most Successful Women Do Differently*, he cites that "strong women do not make the same life choices, but they do end up sharing the same four feelings. They feel successful, an instinctive anticipation, a sense that they are learning and growing and that their most important needs are being met."[12] You see, life isn't about those emotions that cause us pain, grief, and frustration as much as it is about how we choose to handle them and live out our lives. We must choose not to wallow but to live with purpose, confidence, and happiness. Doing so will bring freedom and contentment to our busy, beautiful lives.

Reflections on Your Feelings

On a scale of 1 to 10, how often do you feel guilty in a typical day?

| 1 | 2 | 3 | 4 | 5 | 6 | 7 | 8 | 9 | 10 |

Rarely   A few times   All the time

Who or what in your life causes you to feel guilty? Circle all that apply.

myself	others
spouse	media
children	church

Why do you think these feelings rise up? Is the guilt pointing to another issue in your life?

_____

_____

_____

What changes could you make so that you don't feel guilt as often?

_____

_____

_____

_____

To whom do you compare yourself? Write their names, then write one positive way your personality, strengths, or life circumstances are different from theirs.

What causes you to have FOMO? How can you minimize or eradicate those causes?

What thing or things do you do only because you think you should? Fill out the chart below, paying special attention to the ways you could change this habit, activity, etc. For example, do you have your child in multiple extracurriculars even though the busyness makes you stressed? Could you eliminate an activity from the calendar?

I do this because I think I should	I would like to make this change

What is something you need to let go of? _____

_____

_____

_____

_____

Write down three things you are grateful for today.

1. _____

2. _____

3. _____

Write down three positive words that will remind you of the things you're doing well as a working mother.

1. _____

2. _____

3. _____

Write your purpose statement. _____

_____

_____

_____

FOUR

Practicing Self-Care

With our baby asleep in his crib and my two oldest kids playing a game with their dad, I slipped upstairs for a hot bath and quiet time to read. Baths are my favorite way to nourish my soul, and after a long day at work, I was really looking forward to that time. About twenty minutes into my glorious bath, with the smell of my lavender bath bomb dense in the air, the quiet was disrupted by the sound of little feet running up the stairs. The bathroom door swung open, and I saw both big kids grinning.

Doors mean nothing to children, do they?

My son looked at me, then at my book, and proclaimed, "So, this is what you do in here!"

Sweet mercy. Yes, this is what I do in here—without kids. I laughed and said, "Yes, and Mommy likes to read alone, so get to bed!" The two scampered away, barely closing the door behind them.

Have you ever tried to make time for yourself only to be interrupted by something or someone? In this story, my kids did leave, and I got back to my reading. But it doesn't always go that way.

Prioritizing self-care, which can look like a lot more things than bubble baths, can be difficult for many working moms. I know I have gone through seasons when I pushed my own needs to the bottom of the list. But this happens less often now because I fight for my time. I take naps. I go out with friends. I exercise. Why do I do these things? Because when I take care of myself, I am the best, healthiest version of myself. As working moms, we must subscribe to the oxygen mask philosophy—we have to take care of ourselves by putting on our own oxygen masks before we can effectively take care of others around us.

Seventy-eight percent of the working moms who responded to my survey said that self-care was a struggle for them. I understand the challenges. Pushing aside our own needs to make way for other priorities often feels easier. But when we neglect ourselves, not only do we suffer, but so does everyone else. Eventually, our lack of self-care catches up with us, wreaking havoc in our lives.

A lie many working moms tell themselves is that self-care is selfish. They think that because they are "taking time away for a job" they can't also take time for themselves. This thinking couldn't be farther from the truth. By intentionally investing in ourselves, we are simply declaring our self-worth and proclaiming that who we are as individuals matters. And taking care of ourselves is transformative not only for us personally but also for everyone around us. We cannot teach our children to have their own identities if they see us completely wrapping up our identities in who they are.

Only you can take the steps needed to prioritize yourself and move toward better mental, physical, and spiritual health. Investing in yourself is not selfish. It is necessary. My hope is that this chapter's words and reflection questions will help guide you toward establishing your own regular self-care habits.

Understanding Self-Care

Self-care means different things to different people. For some women, self-care looks like a day of pampering at a spa. For others, it is taking a hike. Still others might equate it with prayer and solitude. In my research of disciplines of self-care, I learned that self-care is all of those things and more. In episode 121 of the popular podcast *The Simple Show*, cohost Tsh Oxenrider referenced Kendra Adachi's definition of self-care as anything that makes you feel more like yourself. I really connected with this simple definition. When someone invests in their own self-care, they are doing what their minds, bodies, and souls need to feel refreshed, alive, and whole.

In the following pages, I break down the practices of self-care into three main areas: mental and emotional care, physical care, and spiritual care. You might find that you need to invest in one area a bit more than the others, and that is completely normal. Be honest with yourself as you read through this chapter, and consider practices you can adopt so that you can be healthier and happier.

Mental and Emotional Care

Have you ever been so busy with work and caring for others that you ended up feeling mentally or emotionally frazzled? When we don't practice proper self-care, our minds experience a never-ending roller coaster of emotions. Unexpected challenges easily push us over the edge when we're feeling stressed. And our good intentions quickly fade when we become angry and impatient with the people we love most. I know that when I work too much and am stretched too thin, I become short-tempered, moody, and not very nice to be around. To mitigate these feelings, we must take time to nurture ourselves mentally and emotionally.

■ Pursue Your Passions

One of the big ways I take care of myself mentally is by making time for my passions—the things I do because they are fulfilling to me alone. Passions are as diverse as the people in the world. Reading, writing, and crafting are three big passions of mine. You might like running, sewing, and cooking. I have found that the what doesn't matter. All that matters is that you create space to do the things you love.

I once heard a former Google employee at a conference share that Google places a great deal of value on sandbox projects. He was talking about something on the side that people do purely for creative expression. For him, it was blogging.

Having something you do for fun is important in creating a healthy, balanced life. I have always been a crafter. Before I had kids, I crafted constantly in my free time. As my career and family have grown, I have had less time to craft. During a particularly busy season, I went so many months without crafting that walking into my craft room caused me to weep. I missed it so much. Something had to change. Now I am doing a better job of making time for those creative hobbies because they are so important to my wellness.

A few weeks before Halloween this year, someone replied to an Instagram story I posted that featured a Halloween costume in progress, saying, "How do you have time to make costumes? For me, a good day is when I am home to make dinner." I replied, "You make time for what's important to you. I skipped chores and worked on costumes." Now, for some, skipping chores is simply not acceptable, but for me, as I have previously admitted, I don't mind. Doing something creative is good for my soul, and when I am soul happy, I am able to do other things with ease and a positive attitude. Truth be told, the week I was making that costume, my workload was brutal and consuming. I was exhausted and fighting to keep my head above water. For that very reason I took time to stop and create, knowing that if I did, I would have enough energy to push through.

When was the last time you lost track of time doing something you love? I asked this question at a conference I spoke at a few years ago, and a woman in the audience raised her hand to answer. She said that the last time she had lost track of time pursuing a passion had been prior to her being a mother. Her oldest was now thirteen. The woman went on to say that it had been so long since she'd taken time to pursue her own passions that she wasn't even sure what she would do if given the time.

If this story resonates with you and you don't know what your passions are or what you would do if you had time to do something you love, think back to your childhood. What did you enjoy doing as a child? Chances are that same thing will still be true for you today. Ever since I learned to read, I've been happy with my nose in a book. This year I made reading a priority and averaged four to five books a month. The activity was so fulfilling!

▥ Journal

Many people find the act of writing to be therapeutic. Licensed professional counselor Kayce Hodos, who has a private practice in Wake Forest, North Carolina, often incorporates this practice into her therapies with working moms. She says that the way in which a woman writes, be it in list form, through a writing app on a phone, or in a journal, doesn't matter. But the act of self-expression can make a huge difference in one's mental health.[1]

If you are interested in journaling, remember there is no right way to do it. But here are a few ideas to get you started:

- *Free-form journal.* This is perhaps the easiest and loosest form of journaling because of its free-form style. In this type of journaling, you literally write down anything that comes to mind. Karen Copp, a registered nurse and mom of two, said, "Journaling for me is a brain dump of ideas, hopes, and dreams. Also, I've used my journal to write out prayers. I find that once I have these thoughts on paper, my mind is clear to focus on home or work tasks that need my attention. Before I started this practice, I felt like my head was so cluttered and scattered. Journaling brings clarity."[2]

- *Prayer journal.* Some women, like Karen, journal as a way to document their prayers. We'll talk a bit more about this in the spiritual self-care section of this chapter.

- *List journal.* Journaling doesn't have to involve lengthy prose. A list journal is just what it sounds like—a journal of lists. Writing lists can help you get your thoughts down in a systemized manner. One year I bought a list journal called *52 Lists.* Each week I made a list based on a list prompt. I looked forward to spending a few minutes during my lunch break documenting everything from what I loved to do outdoors to things I wanted to do in the winter. I enjoyed this process because I am not a big journaler, and the prompts inspired creativity and self-reflection in a fresh way for me. List journaling is very low pressure and can be great for someone who is new to journaling.

- *Gratitude journal.* This form of journaling involves writing down what you are grateful for. Some women prefer to use guided gratitude journals that have a dedicated amount of space for each day, while others prefer to use a blank notebook. Whatever the method, the process of documenting thankfulness in writing has been shown to increase happiness and change a person's outlook. By recording your gratitude, you become in tune with the day's smallest blessings, including things you might have previously overlooked. Reviewing your gratitude journal can also be a useful practice when you are having a difficult day.

- *Electronic journal.* While, traditionally, journaling was done by putting pen to paper, many people now prefer to journal on their computers or their phones. Christina Kirk, scientist and mother of one, shared, "Typically I write emails in Gmail that I don't send. I can type quicker than I write, and I get frustrated writing sometimes. It helps me to flush out what is in my head but not expose it to the world and its repercussions."[3] For some people, electronic journaling allows them to be more free-flowing with their thoughts in the same way Christina described.

▪ Seek Out a Counselor

Sometimes the weight of what we carry is too heavy for us to bear alone. Meeting with a counseling professional can be a helpful way to navigate a challenging time or simply gain some new tools for living life well. Speaking to a professional who can provide input and an unbiased perspective is empowering. Kristen Howerton, a professional writer, counselor, and mom of four, said, "I think that when we are maxed out, our feelings can sometimes run the show, because we don't have the time, margin, or perspective to get a handle on negative thinking patterns. Meeting with a counselor carves that time out and allows us to process things in a more effective way. Processing with another person is cathartic, and there is often value just in speaking our issues out loud."[4]

For some people, getting mental help has a negative stigma. But it shouldn't. As one entrepreneur, a working mom named Kristin, shared, "There is such a stigma to counseling—like if you have to talk to a professional about your problems you are a failure or something. I held it myself for a long time. Today I would advocate everyone to consider it. Find someone you will respect and listen to. Sometimes my counselor told me my feelings were justified. Sometimes I was called out, and I needed to be!"[5]

The benefits of seeing a counselor are broad in scope. A counselor can offer guidance during a tough time, provide tools to help you overcome challenges, and offer an unbiased perspective. For working moms who are often meeting the needs of many other people, counseling can provide a unique kind of respite. Miles Adcox, founder of Onsite, a therapeutic and growth workshop organization, affirms that counseling is beneficial for anyone wanting to learn, heal, and grow.

Counseling is far beyond fixing people's problems; it's opening up people's opportunities. A deeper understanding of who we are and who we are becoming is not what's wrong with us; it's what is right with us. Counseling is often necessary to process adverse life circumstances, trauma, and stress. It's also necessary for the rest of us; both pre- and post-adversity. If you feel stuck or are struggling in any aspect of life, don't wait to reach out. Also, if you want to grow as a human being, leader, parent, etc., counseling is as important an element to human development as education and faith. They all go hand in hand.[6]

Mom and nurse practitioner Nickie shared, "My counseling experience helped me to understand the value of counseling and what it truly is. It is not just sitting there on a couch and talking about your feelings. It is learning why you are thinking the way you are and healthy ways of coping and improving your thought patterns."[7] Teacher and mom of three Amy shared that her family has used counseling services many times over the years, including for marriage guidance and to work through kid issues. She added, "We call them 'family counselors' . . . because they are there to help our family become better and stronger. We benefitted in so many ways—we were able to get an objective opinion on something, we were able to talk through difficult topics, and we were able to have our fears, anxieties, and stresses affirmed by a third party. We always say that the world would be a better place if everyone saw a counselor."[8]

Counseling frequency varies for people depending on their circumstances. Some will choose to see a counselor weekly for a period of time, while others will see a counselor annually to check in and set goals. Whatever the season or the reason, counseling can be an important component of caring for yourself. As working mom Shelley affirmed, "I was able to regroup and breathe when I was at my sessions. Now I am a better person and can take everything that I learned and got out of the sessions and apply it to my everyday life."[9] Realtor and working mom Karen said, "For me, the conversations were very eye-opening and the therapist had a way of asking me questions that helped me to see things from a different perspective. It was also so helpful to have an hour a week where it was just about me! My thoughts, my feelings, my concerns."[10]

The investment of time and energy into seeing a counselor can truly reap rewards that extend throughout your lifetime. Through counseling, many find that they uncover truths they didn't know about themselves, improve their relationships, and learn strategies for living a healthier life.

Mental and emotional self-care isn't a privilege. It's a necessity. Schedule set periods of time in your days and weeks to tend to your needs. Doing so is the only way to ensure consistent investment in yourself.

Physical Care

After my third child was born, I was diagnosed with diastasis recti, which is a stretching or tearing of the abdomen. This often happens after multiple pregnancies and depending on the severity can result in significant lower back pain and/or a hernia. I had a significant tear and was experiencing constant low back pain. When I would bend over, the pain would take my breath away, and I found it difficult to do many daily tasks.

I also had very large breasts, just like my mama and her mama, and had wanted a breast reduction since high school. After nursing my babies, my breasts were gigantic and causing all sorts of neck and shoulder pain as well as chronic headaches.

The combination of these two ailments made me a mess physically. I went to a chiropractor nearly weekly. I was taking migraine medication often. I started seeing a physical therapist in hopes of repairing the diastasis but did not experience relief.

Finally, I said, "Enough is enough. I am not going to continue living like this." I went to a plastic surgeon for a consult. I filled out the paperwork to get approval from my insurance company for a reduction. We saved to pay for an abdominoplasty to repair my abdominal tear and remove the extra skin left from my pregnancies. Ten months later, during one surgery, I had a breast reduction and an abdominoplasty.

That surgery literally changed my life. The physical relief, which I expected, was immediate. The unexpected confidence and emotional impact were just as significant.

The surgery required an investment of time, money, and energy. The recovery was painful, difficult, and slow. Putting it off in the short term, turning my attention to my other responsibilities, would have been easier. But delaying the procedures wasn't doing anyone any good, particularly with me in pain day in and day out. My quality of life was suffering, and that impacted the people around me as well. Taking care of my body's physical needs was important and ultimately made a positive difference for my work, family, and life.

Many women don't worry about their physical health until something dramatic happens. We must shift that mentality and recognize that investing in our health is necessary to being happy and successful.

Have you ever gotten sick because you were doing too much and got run down? This happens to me several times a year. I burn the candle at both ends for far too long, and eventually, destruction happens. My body literally forces me to rest, reminding me that I need to take care of my physical self.

We would never let our children become sick from lack of care. Yet as working moms, we can too easily push our own needs aside, making excuses that we are too busy for annual checkups, dental cleanings, and exercise. We make poor eating choices, don't get enough sleep, and run from one thing to the next with little reprieve. We need to stop that cycle.

Let's review some basic ways you can take care of yourself.

■ Get Regular Checkups

Going to the doctor may not be fun or feel like a necessary priority, but scheduling regular checkups is an important part of being proactive with your health. You should have an annual physical as well as cleanings at the dentist every six months. Also, make a point to get the flu vaccine each year, as this can help to keep you and others well.

To prepare for your appointment, keep a list of questions on your phone. Add to that list whenever you think of a question so that you can use your time with your healthcare provider well.

Please also be aware of guidelines for other screenings such as breast cancer, colon cancer, and cervical cancer, as these vary by age.

If, after your physical, a test comes back abnormal, do not wait to schedule follow-up appointments. The biggest gift you can give yourself and your family is a healthy you. Denying yourself the privilege of seeing a physician is unacceptable.

▪ Pay Attention to Your Body

Our bodies do a good job of letting us know when something is wrong. Pay attention to your body, and respond if something is not normal. Don't ignore it! Doing so will only cause more trouble in the long run.

I have a friend who dealt with debilitating, extremely heavy menstrual periods for years that left her severely anemic before she finally scheduled an ablation. When she went in for the surgery, her iron levels were so low that the medical team was surprised she was able to walk. After years of anemia, not only had her body and brain acclimated to low oxygen levels, but she also had developed a heart murmur due to a lack of iron in her blood. She received a four-liter blood transfusion so she could safely have the ablation, but after the simple, twenty-minute surgical procedure, she slipped into heart failure, which also resulted in severe pneumonia, and she was hospitalized for six days to address the strain on her heart and the pneumonia. Her neglect of her own self-care, what her body had been saying for years, led to life-threatening heart failure.

While this story is extreme, it is a reminder not to ignore your health, blaming inconvenience and more important tasks at hand. Nothing is more important than you!

■ Drink Plenty of Water

Your body is 60 percent water, so it needs plenty of fluids to function properly. Recommendations vary, but you should average around eight eight-ounce glasses of fluids a day. I notice a huge difference when I start my day with a glass of water. If you find it difficult to drink a lot of water, add a flavor packet to a bottle of water. Also, always carry a bottle of water with you so you can drink on the go.

■ Exercise

It comes as no surprise that you should take time to exercise. The Centers for Disease Control and Prevention recommends that adults get at least 150 minutes of physical activity a week.[11]

Many working moms shared with me that they want to work out, but finding the time is incredibly difficult. Start small, and remember that even fifteen minutes here and fifteen minutes there add up.

I long struggled to make time for physical activity. It always seemed to be the first thing I'd cut from my schedule. After being inspired by my husband, I started slow by walking in the early morning, before the kids woke up and the day began. After doing this for a few months, I added in a few classes. I also bought a bike for beneath my desk at work that allows me to pedal my feet while I work. The combination of these three things has made a huge difference in my physical health and also my mental health.

Jess Botte, founder and head coach of JBeWell Fitness Solutions, encourages her clients not to focus on a weight-loss goal.

We focus on getting stronger, feeling less stressed, not feeling as winded when we play, having more energy, and we find ways to quantify that. I've never had a client say they were worse off after adding exercise into their life or that exercise negatively affected them in some way. I find that physical strength equals mental strength. I think that's the biggest win. Strength equals confidence and improved self-worth.[12]

As a working mom, you will need to create exercise habits that work for you. Pediatrician and mom of three Jennifer McHugh-Barker exercises five times a week. With her busy schedule, she finds that using a website that offers free workouts of varying length and difficulty level and running a few times a week with friends give her a great range of activity and time with friends as she takes care of her body.[13]

Our mental health is also impacted by physical activity. Nurse practitioner Nickie Snyder, mother of two, shared:

> When I do not get my workouts, I am easily irritable, distracted, and quite frankly grumpy. My workouts vary from running to boot camps, but it is so important to me that I exercise for at least thirty minutes three to four days per week. This requires planning and discipline to get to bed on time, but it is so worth it for how much better I feel. On top of the health benefits for myself, I'm hoping to set an example for my kids so that they grow up thinking exercise is as normal as breathing.[14]

■ Eat Healthy

A balanced diet that includes plenty of fruits and vegetables, lean protein, and whole grains is best. Try to minimize foods that are processed and high in fat and sugar. Health coach Liza Baker recommends eating SOLE food, which stands for seasonal, organic, local, and ethical. For many of her clients, making this transition isn't easy, so she recommends starting small and making choices to move one step closer to whole foods.[15]

Make choices regarding your meals that enable you to spend less time cooking and preparing, giving you more time to do other things. Make a double batch of dinner so you have leftovers or can freeze some for a later date. Cooking two whole chickens instead of one means you have extra chicken for soup, salads, taco night, and so on. When the grocery store has a sale on ground turkey or beef, I often stock up and prepare it all by browning it, making meatballs, and so on. Then I put the prepared meat in the freezer so that dinner is easy during busy weeks. I love having breakfast hash during the week, but it can be tedious chopping sweet potatoes, onions, red potatoes, and peppers every morning. So I do a lot of chopping all at once on Sunday afternoons, roast two big pans, and I am set for the week. Many working moms create freezer meals, which make meals a snap during busy weeknights. Busy mom and blogger Erin from the blog *Sunny Side Up* grocery shops and preps all her food for the week at once. She bags healthy snacks, making them easy to grab on the go. By taking the time to do this once, she ensures that she and her family have healthy food to eat throughout the week.[16]

Planning meals and snacks ahead of time makes things go smoother day to day, and you will be less likely to make food choices you'll later regret.

◼ Rest

Sleep is critical to overall health. When children are little, we can always tell when they need more sleep. Though we are better able to hide our need for sleep as adults, we still tend to show certain signs when we are tired: irritability, difficulty completing thoughts and sentences, and move at a slower pace.

During a period when I was working a lot of hours, I noticed I was ready for bed by 8:30 p.m. Rather than pushing through and doing more tasks, I listened to my body and went to bed. I am convinced that getting that extra sleep helped keep me healthy during that busy season.

According to the National Sleep Foundation, the average woman should get seven to nine hours of sleep a night.[17] If you are getting less sleep than that, over time it will take a toll on your body physically as well as make things more challenging for you mentally and emotionally. Be sure to adjust your schedule so that you can get optimum sleep each night, even if that means doing less in the evening. You will be a more productive and happier employee, wife, mother, and friend if you are well rested.

Evaluate the choices you are making regarding your physical health and consider where you might need to make changes to take better care of yourself. There is only one you!

Spiritual Care

In her book *The Gifts of Imperfection: Let Go of Who You Think You're Supposed to Be and Embrace Who You Are*, Brené Brown defines "spirituality" as "[the celebration] that we are all inextricably connected to each other by a power greater than all of us." She goes on to say, "Our connection to that power and to one another is grounded in love and compassion. Practicing spirituality brings a sense of perspective, meaning and purpose to our lives."[18]

As a Christian, I can attest to what Brené says about the practice of spirituality. When I'm intentionally engaging my personal connection to God and actively centering that relationship in love and compassion for other people as well as for myself, I'm an all-around healthier and happier individual. That's because spirituality—our connection to God and other people—not only plays an integral part in our ability to be a healthy individual but also is definitive in helping us become the person we were meant to be. Oftentimes when we neglect ourselves, we also neglect our spirituality. We might go through the motions, but we don't experience deep growth.

Spiritual practices are diverse in form—from time spent in a church to walks in nature to reading a daily inspirational book—and are an important part of spiritual care.

■ Meditate and Practice Mindfulness

The act of quieting one's spirit and practicing meditation is a spiritual practice embraced by numerous religious and philosophical traditions. Eastern practices of meditation typically rely on focused breathing or a question to ponder. A more Western, biblical approach would follow the words of Psalm 46:10, which says, "Be still, and know that I am God" (NIV).

One popular form of meditation is mindfulness. I was first introduced to the concept of mindfulness through a workshop at my office. Over the course of a few weeks, I was amazed at how my body's tension and my mind's outlook positively shifted when I worked to be more mindful.

Mindfulness coach Iman Khan explains:

> Mindfulness is really learning to practice to be in the moment in a nonjudgmental way. And the nonjudgment piece is really the key. I think when it comes to working mothers, there is so much pressure, there's so many to-do lists, there's so many responsibilities, and we feel as though we have to please this person and please that person. And mindfulness really teaches you first to take a step back, to create that pause, when you feel something's lacking.[19]

That pause can help you understand people and situations from a perspective other than your own. When you practice mindfulness, you become less likely to see things from only one point of view. This also enables you to see yourself from these other perspectives. You are then able to receive feedback in a gentler manner and become more open to change.

Many books, podcasts, and seminars teach mindfulness, but it basically involves practicing being still and alert at the same time. Here are some tips to get you started:

- *Set aside some time.* Mindfulness doesn't require any special equipment, chairs, or cushions. You simply need to set aside the time in your busy day to practice it.

- *Observe the present moment as it is.* The goal of mindfulness is not a state of calmness or quieting of the mind, though that does often happen. The goal is simply to pay attention to your present, without judgment and without letting your mind wander. For many working moms, this lack of judgment is the tough part.

- *Let your judgments roll by.* If you notice judgments creeping in while you're practicing mindfulness, make a mental note of them, and then let them pass. This is not the time to analyze them.

- *Return to observing the present moment as it is.* Your mind may easily get distracted by all the things you have to do, which is why mindfulness involves repeatedly returning to the present moment.

- *Be kind to your wandering mind.* Show yourself kindness, and don't judge the thoughts that creep in. Instead, recognize where your mind wanders off to and gently bring your attention back to the present.[20]

That's it!

Though mindfulness appears to be simple, it does take a lot of practice. You might find some mindfulness apps helpful as you journey toward consistent mindfulness. Some popular options include:

- Headspace
- Smiling Mind
- iMindfulness
- Mindfulness Daily

▪ Read Spiritual Books

Another way to foster spiritual growth is to read spiritual books that resonate with you. The study of spirituality and spiritual practices to deepen one's faith is centuries old. In my own life, I have found that the words of others and the stories of their faith journeys have increased my own faith and shaped my beliefs. For instance, Ann Voskamp's book *One Thousand Gifts* taught me to see life through a lens of gratitude. Emily Freeman's book *A Million Little Ways* was transformative in my perspective about God, art, and creativity. As an avid reader, I find that spiritual books minister to me in profound ways.

Taking time to read the Bible is another effective way to nurture your spirituality. Often I find that when I open my Bible, the words minister directly to my life circumstances. The more I study and learn its words, the more ways I am able to apply its truths to my life.

▪ Keep a Prayer Journal

We talked earlier about how journaling can be a helpful practice for mental and emotional health. Prayer journaling, in particular, can also be beneficial for your spiritual health.

For many working moms, the biggest benefit of a prayer journal is that the act of writing reduces distractions and increases focus. Through prayer journaling, people are able to focus on their relationship and communion with God. Writing is a slower process than speaking, so it can make the art of prayer more meaningful.

A prayer journal can also help you document your faith journey. Looking back and seeing prayers that were answered can be encouraging.

Writing in a prayer journal can also be a useful way to document what you are reading in the Bible. Journaling through Scripture helps to improve understanding and retention.

▪ Gather with Other People

Being in community can be deeply spiritual. Gathering with other people might also be a way to encourage your faith. This can happen in a place of worship or simply over coffee with a group of like-minded people of faith. For instance, many churches offer community or home groups designed specifically to help people engage with one another beyond Sunday mornings.

That said, for some people, these types of events are draining. For instance, after trying out several community groups through our church, my husband and I realized that a weekly gathering was adding stress to our lives and was not something we looked forward to. So we opted not to participate. And that is okay! For friends of ours, their community group has been a lifeline to them, and they can't imagine it not being a part of their week. Spiritual practices should not be forced, so it is important to recognize what best ministers to you.

If you long for spiritual community but are not connected with a spiritual body, many retreat centers offer opportunities for gathering together. Whether a daylong seminar on meditation or a weeklong intensive on faith, these types of workshops can be like water to a dry, stretched-too-thin soul.

Consider these spiritual practices—and others—and decide what habits you need to nurture to ensure spiritual health.

Prioritizing and Practicing Self-Care

Focusing on your family and career is not enough. You must take time to practice self-care. Don't become so busy that you forget to love yourself well. Doing so is going to make you a better wife, mom, co-worker, and friend.

If you are someone who finds it challenging to prioritize self-care, schedule time for yourself in the same way you schedule meetings at work. Put going to the gym, gathering with friends, or having a quiet lunch by yourself on your calendar. You may also want to consider having a friend hold you accountable so you do not push yourself aside. These simple acts can ensure that you take care of you.

Today I hope you take a close look at the ways you are making time for yourself as well as any adjustments you might need to make. And if you haven't been to the doctor in a while, call and schedule an appointment!

Reflections on Your Self-Care

What do you currently do to maintain good mental health?

_____

_____

_____

_____

In what ways do you neglect your mental health? _____

_____

_____

_____

When you think of your passions, what immediately comes to mind? If it has been a long time since you made time for your passions, consider what you enjoyed doing as a child and if that would have relevance to you as an adult.

_____

_____

_____

_____

Taking care of your physical health includes several habits. Consider the following practices and make notes about the areas in which you are doing well and in which you need to improve:

regular checkups	
water intake	
exercise	
healthy eating	
rest	

What faith-nurturing activities do you regularly practice? Which would you like to do more?

_____

_____

_____

Are there certain times of the day when you feel most open to spiritual care? If so, how can you better use that time?

_____

_____

_____

_____

If you neglect yourself when life gets busy, think of something else you could sacrifice instead. For instance, instead of making a home-cooked meal, maybe you could get takeout or keep things simple with sandwiches and fruit. Write down three ideas for simplifying your life during busy times so you can continue to make yourself a priority.

FIVE

Finding Rhythm at Work

Undoubtedly, your work looks different from mine. I work in marketing; you might be a physician. I work in an office; you might work in a store or at home. But we are alike in that we have a big responsibility beyond our family—and that is a job we are paid to do.

I remember finding out I was pregnant in 2007 and being overcome with joy while also immediately wondering about my job. The agency I worked at had very few parents on staff. Not working wasn't an option for me both because I loved my work and because it wasn't financially feasible for our family. So I had no choice but to do what millions of other mothers do—make a job and family work together. For me, that looked like picking a day care near my office so I could breastfeed on my lunch break. It meant leaving work at 5:20 every day, not a minute later, so I could get to day care on time for pickup. It also meant my husband and I had to structure life to ensure we had quality time with our son, with each other, and for the things we loved.

Our family and my career grew in tandem. When I got pregnant with our second child, people asked if I would stop working. I said no. But at that time, I recognized I did want to find a job that had a slower pace than the demanding agency I was at. I didn't expect to make a move until I was on maternity leave, but when an opportunity arose a few months into my pregnancy, I took the leap. At six months pregnant, I gave notice.

That day was incredibly hard. I remember going into the office manager's office, closing the door, and crying that I had gotten another job and needed to give my notice to the company's CEO. The office manager teared up too but kindly said, "Sometimes, Jess, you have to do hard things."

She was right, and while leaving was terribly hard, it was the best decision for me both personally and professionally. The job I accepted that day in March 2011 is the one I am still at seven years later.

Life today in my current job is very different, but it's a good different. Instead of long hours and lots of travel, I am able to leave work at work and be home more. I love the people I work with. They have taught me so much about what community at work can really look like. They laugh and work hard. They are supportive of my other passions and love my children.

I share that story because I think it really shows the tension we feel as working moms. We can be happy in a job, and yet it may not be the right fit for our family. We can love our co-workers and still want to leave work at work. Embracing my life as a professional while recognizing that it is just one of my many "hats" has brought much peace and satisfaction to my life. Having a clear sense of what work is to you and the weight you want it to have in your life is critical.

Understanding Your Why

I am proud to call myself a working mom. I love my work and believe that the work I do has value. When I think about other working moms I know, the reasons why each works vary. I asked a few why they worked, and here are some of their answers:

"I love using my brain."

"I like being challenged at work."

"I help provide for my family."

"It makes me a happier person and a better wife and mom."

"I feel like the work I do is important work."

"I work because I have two kids to pay for, though I don't love my profession."

"I work to help provide for the family and take some burden off my husband."

"I work because I feel like it keeps my mind sharp."

"I work because I love to work and socializing with my colleagues."

"I love using my degree and certification."

"I'm the primary breadwinner in my family."

"So I have 'something' once the kids are gone."

"Because I am more than a mom."

Understanding the why behind your work can help you navigate the challenges a career brings. In addition, your why speaks to the way you perceive your work. Dr. Amy Wrzesniewski, an associate professor of organizational behavior at Yale University's School of Management, outlined a helpful classification system of the ways in which people orient their work. A *Psychology Today* article describing Wrzesniewski's research defined the orientations as follows:

> *Job orientation.* Individuals who fall into this category tend to view their work as a means to an end. They work to receive the pay and/or benefits to support their hobbies, families, or life outside work. They prefer jobs that do not interfere with their personal lives. They are not as likely to have a strong connection to their workplaces or their job duties. The job serves as a basic necessity in life.

Career orientation. Individuals with a career orientation are
more likely to focus on elements related to success or
prestige. They are more interested in the ability to move
upward in their careers, to receive raises and new titles,
and to achieve the social standing that comes from the
careers. Careers that have a clear upward "ladder" are appealing to those with a career orientation.

Calling orientation. Individuals with a calling orientation
often describe their work as integral to their lives and
their identity. They view their careers as a form of self-
expression and personal fulfillment. They are more likely
to find their work meaningful and will modify their duties
and develop relationships to make it more so. They are
more satisfied in general with their work and their lives.[1]

Which of these orientations fits your perspective toward your
work? There isn't a right answer here. Understanding your orientation can help you understand your outlook toward your work as
well as the passions and pitfalls it brings.

Recognizing the Value of Your Work

Work has many benefits, but seeing them is not always easy. Sometimes our jobs can seem like, well, work, and so we forget all the
positive things they bring to our lives. Considering the following
benefits can help you remember your work's value even on the
hard days.

Financial Benefit

Most women work to help provide for their families. In fact,
in 40 percent of households, mothers are now the sole or primary
income providers.[2] Women's financial contribution is significant
for today's families, and the financial impact extends beyond bank

accounts to health care and other benefits provided by employers. For my family, my day job affords us financial stability, healthcare benefits, college tuition benefits, a 401(k), discounts for local businesses, and so much more.

Opportunity to Use Your Talents

Work gives you an opportunity to use your gifts in a way that is likely different from how you use them at home. I have always had a knack for selling things, and this is a gift I am able to bring to my career in marketing. If I were a stay-at-home mom, I wouldn't have the same opportunities to flex my marketing muscles, and those gifts would likely atrophy from little use. My friend Melissa is a florist. While she can use her gift to make gorgeous flower arrangements for her home, her work allows her to extend the beauty of that gift to weddings, special events, and more. As a result, thousands are touched by her stunning floral art.

Friendship

Work can also offer emotional stability through the friendships—and adult conversations—you can find there. When I had surgery in 2016, my work friends rallied, bringing my family meals for two weeks. They were the first at the hospital to meet my babies and know more about my day-to-day world than anyone else in my life. Work friends can be one of the biggest blessings of a career. Later on, in the friendship chapter, we'll spend some time further unpacking the value of work friendships.

Service to Others

Depending on your job, you might also find that your work helps you contribute to society in a way that is meaningful to you. I do marketing for a large hospital system, and I find sharing health information that can positively impact a person's life incredibly rewarding. In my writing and speaking career, I am humbled to know that my words might help a woman live a happier, more fulfilled life. I love how working mom Melinda, who works for a physician negotiating insurance coverage for patients, put it: "There is nothing like a patient getting what they need and starting to feel better!"[3] Many careers afford women the opportunity to serve people.

Positive Impact on Your Kids

The impact of your work on your kids can also be significant and positive. Not only does time together become more precious and valued, but your work also impacts the way your children will grow up and approach their own work and families. A study conducted by Kathleen L. Mcginn, Cahners-Rabb Professor of Business Administration at Harvard Business School (HBS), along with HBS researcher Mayra Ruiz Castro and Elizabeth Long Lingo, an embedded practitioner at Mt. Holyoke College, showed that "women whose moms worked outside the home are more likely to have jobs themselves, are more likely to hold supervisory responsibility at those jobs, and earn higher wages than women whose mothers stayed home full time, according to a new study. Men raised by working mothers are more likely to contribute to household chores and spend more time caring for family members."[4] Basically, your work can be good for your kids and will impact the way they live and raise their families.

▪ Teaching Your Children the Value of Work

Your work teaches your kids the importance of responsibility and what it means to contribute to an organization and to society. As a working mom, you are able to model a strong work ethic and ways to manage multiple responsibilities. Though my children are young, they understand that sometimes you have to work before you play. A working mom named Kris said, "My husband and I try to explain to our boys (fifteen and eleven) that even though we love what we do, sometimes work is just work. You still do it. It doesn't have to be fun all the time. You aren't going to get warm fuzzies and a parade every day. Sometimes you just have to put your head down and work."[5]

Your work also demonstrates for your children how to work toward goals in a healthy manner. As researcher Leslie Forde shared, "I'm trying to show my children that they can be high-achieving, have a high bar, and care about what they're doing, but without eating themselves up if it takes them time to find the right tools to reach their goal."[6]

▪ Teaching Your Children the Value of Play

Outside of work, your children witness that it is important to make space for other things, including play. Work should not mean that they don't see you pursuing other activities. Instead, it should provide a way for your children to see how these pursuits can fit in with a career. I don't hide my passions from my children. I invite them in. We spend many nights reading together in our master bedroom, tucked in layers of blankets on our king-sized bed. While our tastes in literature are obviously different, our love of books is not.

Finding Success in Your Work

While women participate in many kinds of work, certain practices can be applied to numerous careers that result in success in that work. It's important to note here that my definition of success in the workplace isn't about climbing the corporate ladder. Rather, it's about being satisfied in and with your work.

The researcher I mentioned earlier in this chapter, Dr. Amy Wrzesniewski, promotes the practice of "job crafting," in which people make the jobs they have the jobs they love. "The evidence— gathered from studies on organizations as varied as Fortune 500 companies and tiny nonprofits—suggests that people who do this tend to be more satisfied and engaged in their work, perhaps because what they do all day at their jobs has become more closely aligned with their most dearly held beliefs about what makes life enjoyable, or meaningful."[7]

Much of the following advice can help you create a job you love. If your job isn't fulfilling, the following ideas can help you reconfigure it into one that is more engaging and aligned with your skills, goals, and desires. With that in mind, I encourage you to consider the following practices to see how they could benefit you in your life. (Some of the advice that follows is specific to office culture, but most is applicable for women who do any type of work.)

Establish Work Boundaries

Boundaries at work lead to job satisfaction, strong relationships, and successful completion of tasks. Yet they can be incredibly difficult to create and maintain. When we lack boundaries, we often find ourselves feeling overwhelmed and stretched too thin.

Regardless of whether you work at home or in an office, retail setting, restaurant, or factory, developing boundaries begins with establishing ground rules for what you want your work life to look like. All work environments are different, so you will need to think about what makes the most sense for your place of employment. Some things you might consider include:

- What hours do you work? Are these the best for your family, or would working a different shift be to your and your family's benefit?
- Do you have a lunch break? If so, how are you using it? Are you eating at a desk or stepping away and truly getting a break?
- Do you often work overtime? If so, is this out of financial necessity, for job security, or for another reason? Could

you talk with your boss about having a more manageable workload?

- Do certain people negatively impact the way in which you work? How can you manage these relationships so that the impact is not negative?

Earlier in my career, I wasn't bold enough to set clear boundaries. I am a hard worker, and no matter what was asked of me, I did the work. This often meant checking and responding to emails both day and night. It also meant that, even if my workload was excessive, I would take on more and never say no to my superiors or to a client.

Eventually, I realized this wasn't a healthy way to work. Though creating healthy boundaries was uncomfortable at first, I became committed to doing so. I was honest about my workload. I changed jobs to work at a place where I could leave work at work and focus on my family at home. I said no often.

Once you've established healthy boundaries, technology can help you maintain those boundaries. For instance, try putting your phone on silent or leaving it on a table when you are home and don't want to be distracted by the email pings. Invest in lighting that automatically goes off at a certain time so that you don't continue to work. You can also download plug-ins and web browser extensions that will prevent selected websites like social media from distracting you. All these things can help you maintain boundaries in your work.

Speak Up

Recently, my office went through a remodel, which was a very big deal because in addition to new carpet and desks, the seating chart was radically changed. More people were placed in offices together, and teams were shaken up. Initially, the management team was leading this effort, and the rest of the people in the office felt very much in the dark. After hearing feedback from fellow co-workers who were concerned about the changes, I decided to speak up for the group and ask if I could be added to the task force for the remodel. I felt I could advocate for my co-workers and help move the project forward in a positive manner.

You may have similar examples of times you advocated for others, working to ensure positive results. Yet too often we are unwilling to advocate in the same way for ourselves. Recognizing if this is a stumbling block is very important, because speaking up regarding our best interests, workloads, conflicts, and the like creates a healthier, happier work environment.

For instance, at one point during a weekly meeting with my supervisor, I decided to talk with her about challenges I was having with my workload. I took a deep breath and shared how the projects I had been given were too much for me to handle without some help. I explained that, due to my workload, I could not complete them all in a timely fashion without a significant increase in the hours I was working, which was not something I was willing to commit to. After honestly evaluating the tasks at hand, my supervisor and I began discussing ways to prioritize the work, and we even outlined some opportunities for delegation. Leaving that meeting, despite still having a full plate, I felt better and more empowered because I had spoken my frustrations aloud.

Was this a difficult conversation to have? Sure. But it was far less difficult because I had developed a healthy and candid rapport with my supervisor. She respects me, and she not only trusts me to be honest but also expects it. This is not something that happened overnight, of course. All relationships take time, even those in the workplace.

When you need to address a conflict, a challenge, or a shift in scope of work, don't be afraid to speak up. But when you do, be prepared, especially if you are meeting with your supervisor. Preparation will reduce some possible nervousness about the conversation and help you go into the meeting focused on the desired outcome.

Take Time Off

A 2017 survey by careers website Glassdoor found that the average US employee who receives paid vacation takes only about half (54 percent) of the days they are allotted in a year. The biggest reasons offered for not taking vacation days revolved around fear—fear of being replaced, of having too much work to do after vacation, etc.[8]

For many working moms, vacation days are gobbled up by family related activities, both good things like vacations and not-so-good things like a sick child. The idea of a true break is just that—an idea. But if you are in a position where vacation days are available, work toward maximizing some of those days for refreshment and self-care. Days off are available because employers know that they benefit both employees and the workplace.

I am ruthless about taking vacation days and never leave any on the table. I schedule days off every month, set my out-of-office message, and do my thing. I also try not to look at email because doing so can reduce my vacation experience. If I will be checking email while I'm away, I still say that I won't be to ensure that no one has expectations of my accessibility. My boss often will take email off her phone to enable her to really step away from work while on vacation.

I find that time away from the office makes me a better, more creative employee. Sure, the emails pile up, and the first day or two after a vacation can be busy while I'm catching up, but the time away is always worth it.

Sometimes you might need an extended vacation or sabbatical. Two years ago, I took a one-month break from blogging—my first in ten years. I realized that if I didn't stop, my business, my personal life, and my future would suffer. At the beginning of the break, I didn't know what to do with myself. I was so used to waking up early and working that I would open my computer and just mindlessly flip through Facebook.

Thankfully, on that Saturday, a book arrived. It was an advanced copy sequel to a book I'd devoured earlier in the month. I read the entire thing in a morning, and it provided what I needed to push the blog aside. When I told my sister Melissa that I had read an entire book that morning, she asked, "Are you just loving your life? Do you ever want to blog again?" I replied yes and yes, though I knew I wanted it to look different in the future. Fewer deadlines. More writing from my heart and less writing because of a contract.

A friend once told me that she was going to take time off from her blog to work on a book. I told her that was foolish. How was she going to sell a book if she didn't write on her blog? I realize now that I was the fool. I had believed a lie that taking a break would be blogging career suicide. The truth is that taking breaks can be the healthiest thing we can do for ourselves and can impact our work in far more positive than negative ways.

One woman I interviewed, Keisha Blair, author and cofounder of Aspire-Canada, become a widow after having her second child. After Keisha struggled for several months after her husband's passing, her brother advised her to take a sabbatical outside Canada, where she lives. She selected Jamaica, and the time away gave her new perspective and an awakening. "In essence, what the sabbatical gave me was the power of 'pause' when I was stretched too thin," said Keisha. "I needed a longer pause because I was about to make permanent life changes (as a result of becoming widowed). Decisions like staying in the same home, city, or changing my career as a single parent were top of mind. I think the length of the pause has to be in direct correlation with the time needed to achieve what needs to be done."[9]

Another working professional, Jenni, works as an independent contractor for a literary agency. After years of keeping her plate very full, she ascertained that she needed to change the rhythm of her work. She first experimented with self-imposed breaks from work and technology, such as no internet on Sundays and no weekend office work, then moved into taking longer breaks, such as no major work between Thanksgiving and New Year's and taking the month of July off. She shared:

> Sometimes it is a hard-core sabbatical break, like when my husband and I took the kids to Italy and spent a month living in a tiny Tuscan village; or when we go to the family cabin in the mountains for a week every July—there's no Wi-Fi or electricity, or plumbing for that matter! Other times I still keep office hours; they're just fewer and dedicated to annual tasks such as end-of-year reviews, accounting, and goal setting. Either way, I no longer feel bashful about taking time off for me, because I know the positive difference it makes in my soul and achievements. I plan ahead, set up my out-of-office email reply, and turn my attention to other important matters.

Jenni went on to say, "I have found that practicing Sabbath and sabbatical breaks gives me incredible renewed clarity. I've grown much better at knowing how to quiet my mind, the tyranny of the urgent. When all that noise and pressure is tuned out, I am able to hear and attend to what's going on in my heart. My business is thriving, and I'm enjoying my family life immensely because I've carved out space to invest myself strategically."[10]

Depending on your work, an extended sabbatical like Jenni's or Keisha's may not be possible for you. But I hope their stories inspire you to think about your own practices and to take time off to renew yourself.

Find Flexibility and Make Your Schedule Work

Having flexibility increases working mothers' satisfaction because they are better able to do the things they want to do while still maintaining a career. Research has shown that working moms are better able to navigate work, family, and home when they have flexibility at work. Gallup cites that of the workplace benefits it studied,

"Flextime yielded the strongest relationship to overall wellbeing among employees. Engaged employees with a lot of flextime had 44% higher wellbeing than actively disengaged employees with very little to no flextime."[11]

Flexibility can look different for different women and different professions. It might mean working from home one day a week so that you can volunteer at your child's school midday or splitting a day in half so that you can attend soccer practice at 4:00 p.m. Flexibility can also involve the hours you work in an entire week instead of just a single day. Maybe you work two twelve-hour days instead of three eight-hour days. For some working moms, preparing for the workweek on the weekend can make things flow easier during the week and give them the flexibility they need.

Flexibility has been incredibly important for me in my years as a working mom. I have gone into the office at 7:00 a.m. so I could leave early for my kids' music programs. I have also worked from home at times, which not only saved me up to sixty minutes of commute time but also allowed me to get laundry done on my lunch break and pick my children up from school, which is something my husband normally does. When I work from home, I have fewer interruptions than I do in the office, making me a more productive employee.

Sales executive Sabrina found flexibility by arranging her work schedule so that she would be working while her daughter attended a required school event. Doing this gave her more time with her daughter. She shared, "Did I want to work Friday night? Not really, but I'd rather work when she is not at home than both of us missing each other."[12]

In her book *I Know How She Does It: How Successful Women Make the Most of Their Time*, Laura Vanderkam shares that most women who participated in her research study applied the following strategies to find flexibility:

- *Split shifts.* Some women work until 4:00 p.m. and then do an hour of work later in the evening. By splitting time, women are able to be present for more things with their families.
- *Working remotely.* Some work at home instead of at the office, allowing them to have more time for family and other responsibilities.
- *The 168-hour option.* This option involves the total hours available in a week instead of in a twenty-four-hour period. Some women choose to work longer but fewer days and then have more hours with their families during "prime times."
- *Rethinking weekends.* Some working moms work on the weekend (even for just a short amount of time), which allows them to be more prepared and present for the workweek ahead.[13]

Some companies are more supportive than others when it comes to flexible schedules. When my employer pulled back on the flexibility given to employees, my department saw a significant number of talented colleagues leave for other jobs. In speaking with those former colleagues in the months after, I found that they were all happier to have more flexibility in their new positions. One had taken a job working from home for a big company in California. While she was still putting in the same number of hours, having the flexibility to be present whenever her children needed her made changing jobs worthwhile.

I believe that employers who don't offer flex time or work-from-home options when possible will eventually find it difficult to hire the best people for needed positions. If your current job doesn't allow for a flexible schedule but you feel it is something you desire, consider seeking an opportunity that would afford you more flexibility.

Cultivate Community

Whether you work part-time or full-time, inside the home or outside of it, you need community in your work. Who are the people you can talk to about family and life? Who can you go to when you have a health emergency? Who can you trust?

I'll never forget how alone I felt after first leaving the agency where I started my career and starting my new job. I would cry to my husband at night, saying, "I just want to be known." It took time, but eventually I made friends. I felt safe and trusted. But I realized that I needed more—and so did my colleagues.

So I started organizing Friday potlucks every four to six weeks. It's remarkable to me how food brings people together, especially when it involves recipes that people love to make and share. The office became warmer and more fun. People felt loved and celebrated. Friendships and trust deepened. And morale improved.

Community is a beautiful gift that's worth seeking out at work. It can make your days more joyful and your work experience richer. The people you work with make a big difference in your job's culture and the way you feel about your job. Finding community in the workplace will give you the support you need to thrive at work.

Community isn't something that typically happens instantaneously, and you might need to step out of your comfort zone to find it. Consider looking for ways to cultivate friendship and community in the workplace, perhaps through projects, lunches, extracurricular activities, or simply conversations around the proverbial watercooler. Enjoying the people you work with will have a positive impact on the work you do and your outlook on your job itself.

If finding community in your job is difficult, consider other ways you could find that support. Local networking organizations may introduce you to like-minded individuals and provide the professional outlet you need for friendship.

Utilize Productivity Hacks

When you're feeling stretched too thin at work, it's often because you have more work than can be accomplished during the typical workday. Here are some productivity hacks to help you get the most out of your workday:

- *Make a list.* When you document what you need to accomplish, you are more likely to follow through with those tasks. Many professionals find it helpful to make a list for the week, on either Friday afternoon or Monday morning. This list gives them direction for their work and helps ensure productivity.

- *Turn off email.* Email is an incredible distraction. So shut down Outlook or close your Gmail tab. You will then be able to focus on the task before you without getting sidetracked by that pesky ding. Depending on your work environment, you might need to communicate with your colleagues that you are no longer leaving your email open all day but instead will be checking it periodically. Encourage them to call you or use an office messaging service if they need to reach you immediately. While turning off email might be challenging at first, it will likely increase your productivity and allow you to finish your work in a timelier manner. You will also notice that you are able to be more focused on the work you are doing.

- *Schedule time for specific projects.* In some professions, work calendars can often fill up with meetings, leaving you little time to actually do the work you need to do. Block time on your calendar for accomplishing projects so that you won't be booked for more meetings. This will help ensure that you get your work completed on time.

- *Work off-site.* This goes back to flexibility. Many times if you work outside the office, you are better able to focus on projects and reduce distractions. You end up being more productive than if you were in the office. A Gallup study actually showed that remote workers "log more hours at their primary job than do their on-site counterparts."[14]

- *Talk*. When possible, instead of emailing back and forth, walk to a colleague's office or use chat technology like Skype for Business or Slack to discuss a project. Talking will eliminate unnecessary emails and time spent conversing at length about something that could be cleared up quickly. This does not mean you should sit and talk for extended periods of time about your favorite television show, as that will be counterproductive to saving time.

- *Use technology*. Technology can be incredibly useful, particularly when you are managing a team. Look at tools such as Trello for keeping up with deadlines; Hootsuite, Sprinklr, or Buffer for social media management; and Dropbox or Google Drive for file management. These tools and systems help ensure you don't waste time researching files, doing busy work, and unnecessarily following up with colleagues about work they are doing.

- *Delegate*. Everything does not have to fall on your shoulders. When doing so makes sense, consider delegating work to another colleague or freelancer. This will allow you to be more productive at doing the things only you can do. It also gives you the opportunity to let someone else do work that will help them grow or use their skills.

- *Set meeting time limits*. Meetings can eat up a lot of time in a workday. Always start your meetings on time, and don't allow for chatter at the beginning. Set meeting time limits, and stick to them. If necessary, use a timer. People might chuckle at first, but you will be surprised by how a time limit helps keep a group focused. As you and your team get better at sticking to a time limit, consider reducing your meeting times by 25 percent. Many hour meetings can get done in forty-five minutes if everyone stays on task.

Use Work Travel to Your Advantage

Not all careers require travel, but if you need to travel for your work, look at it as a benefit. (If you don't travel, feel free to skip this section.) I have talked with working moms who get very stressed, sad, or weighed down by feelings of guilt over being away. Preparation and embracing the trip as an opportunity instead of a headache can make a world of difference.

While I can't share an exhaustive list about preparing for work travel because each situation is different, many of the benefits of travel are pretty universal. Here is a list of a few top benefits for working moms:

- *Catch up on work.* Travel offers a great opportunity to catch up on emails that have gotten buried in your inbox, make a list of pending projects, or simply tackle projects that have been waiting in the wings for when you have time. Use your flights and/or time in your hotel to focus on these tasks. Doing so will relieve pressure for when you are back at home.

- *Enjoy time alone.* Work travel is an opportunity for you to get extended periods alone and without interruption. When I travel, I savor that time, using it to pour into myself. I order room service, read books, write, and quiet my soul. Don't feel like you have to work nonstop because you are traveling. Instead, recognize that the trip is a way to get reenergized while you are away from your usual day-to-day responsibilities.

- *Explore a new city.* If your travel takes you to somewhere you have never been, try to make time to enjoy and explore the area. For instance, when I had to travel to Boston for a conference, I took a half day off of work so I could fly in the night before and have time to do a bit of sightseeing. This was my first time in the city, and I wasn't going to miss the chance to see some of it. Yes, this meant I had to leave my family a bit earlier than absolutely necessary, but since I was leaving anyway, it was an easy decision. My husband always encourages me to extend a trip a bit, knowing how much this brings me joy and the way that positively impacts our family. If you don't have time to plan for sightseeing in advance, the app GPSmycity offers walking tours that allow you to see what an area has to offer.

- *Connect with your kids in a new way.* Instead of seeing work travel as stressful, consider it an opportunity to love your kids in a new way. For instance, Jessica, a convention planner and mom of two, takes a Lego figure with her from her son. She then photographs the figure in the city where she is. The photos have become a great source of connection for her and her son. Work travel also allows your kids to miss you and you to miss them, making for sweet reunions. As the old adage says, "Absence makes the heart grow fonder."

- *Give the gift of quality time with someone else.* Work travel also gives your kids quality time with their other parent or someone else who cares for them while you are gone. My husband will often plan a special dinner out or a movie night when I am gone. When we once both had to be out of town for work, my mom visited from out of state to care for the kids. They didn't even want us to come home!

Understanding Your Work's Impact at Home

Your happiness at work directly affects your happiness at home.

One Saturday I spent the day at my office working on a big writing project. I then went to Sam's Club, came home, and spent an hour putting everything away and making dinner. When I finally flopped on the couch, something my son Elias said caused me to snap at him in response. My husband looked at me and said, "I realize you're tired from working all day, but don't take it out on him." He was right. I apologized to Elias and pulled him in for a snuggle. I don't want to be a mom with a short fuse.

The next day I again spent a chunk of time working at my office, but when I came home, I was different. I came home ready to be a mom. During my drive home, I mentally prepared myself for the next part of my day. I stopped thinking about work. I turned my attention to what I wanted to do at home and what my kids would need from me. None of these thoughts were incredibly deep or spiritual, but they were enough to ensure that my attitude was kind and loving toward my family. As I walked in the door, I flipped my phone to silent and left it on the hall table. That night I played chess with my eldest son, colored with my daughter, and read my littlest a story. I went to bed content with the way my day had gone. I had both achieved my goals at work and spent quality time with my family.

If you're celebrating the benefits of being a working mom and pursuing practices that will help you find success in the workplace, your home life will reap the benefits as well. These intentional choices have the power to make you a better employee, a healthier individual, and a more loving parent and spouse. So boldly choose to make them every day.

Reflections on Your Work

Why do you work?

Work has many benefits. Reflect on and write down at least three benefits your work brings to your life and family.

Which job orientation fits your perspective toward your work: job orientation, career orientation, calling orientation?

On a scale of 1 to 10, how good are you at establishing boundaries in your work?

Consider your current workload. Is there something that could be scaled back? If so, write down some action steps to make that happen. _____

_____

_____

_____

How often do you take a vacation? Do you use all your vacation days each year? _____

_____

_____

How do you currently use your lunch break? _____

_____

_____

What tools can keep you organized in your work? _____

_____

_____

_____

Do you currently have any flexibility in your job? If not, make a list of possible ways your job could be flexible and plan a time to speak with your boss. If so, are you using those flexible benefits wisely? What shifts in your schedule could you make so that you have increased flexibility?

_____

_____

_____

_____

Are you where you want to be in your career? If not, list any short- or long-term goals for the future.

_____

_____

_____

What is your community like at work? List three ways you could deepen that community (i.e., plan a potluck, surprise someone with a handwritten card, invite a colleague out to lunch). Pick one of those three ideas and act on it this week.

_____

_____

_____

_____

Review this chapter's productivity hacks. Which ones can you adopt in your own life to be more productive?

_____

_____

_____

SIX

Investing in Your Marriage

Let me start by saying that I know this chapter is not fit for everyone. If you are a single mom, I esteem you very much. The responsibilities and additional tensions you have to deal with are incredible. I hope you will find a lot of value in this book's other chapters.

I felt including a chapter on marriage was important, though, because two-thirds of the moms who filled out my survey said that marriage or making time for their spouse or significant other was a challenge for them. Here is a sampling of some of those comments:

My husband and I are so busy and tired that we "forget" to pay attention to each other.

Having both my husband and I working leads me to feel that we lead separate lives, and communication becomes a challenge on top of the general difficulty in making time for "us."

After I give emotionally all day at work, then come home to cook/clean for us and take care of the majority of kid-related things, I don't have much left in my tank to give my husband. I know he gets the short end of the stick, but I still haven't figured out a way to balance everything.

I feel as if I have become a roommate to my husband. I love and adore him, but I have no energy left after taking care of the kids. I miss him dearly, but I feel as if I have nothing left to give.

My husband and I find it difficult to find time to have any sort of conversation outside of work and kids.

Did those comments resonate with you? Many of them ring true for me. Here's how a normal day looks for our family. Typically, my husband and I both wake up early. Matthew watches the news, and I usually write for about an hour. The kids are all up by 6:00, and we turn our attention to getting everyone and everything ready for the day. Matthew leaves to take the kids to school at 7:35, and I usually leave by about 8:00. He picks up the kids at 4:30, comes home, and starts dinner. I get home at 5:30. We then spend time together as a family. We eat dinner, do homework, give baths, read stories, play games, and then get ready for bed. On a perfect night, all the kids are in bed by 8:00, but oftentimes it ends up being 8:15 or 8:20. At that point, I want to collapse. Usually, I'll take a little time to clean up or put laundry away and then read before bed—if I can keep my eyes open. Matthew and I will sometimes hang out together, but typically, we are both so tired that we often just need to do our own thing to decompress from the day.

Being a working mom has so many variables that make it difficult, and they extend beyond your roles as a mom and a co-worker. Being a wife who is engaged, loving, and patient takes real work. Coasting in your marriage sometimes feels easier than really investing it in. But what I have learned is that I need my husband—and not just to help divvy up chores and kid responsibilities. I need his love, friendship, and attention. When our relationship is thriving, so are all the other areas of my life.

Matthew and I have had our share of mountains and valleys in our fourteen years of marriage. He is my biggest cheerleader, and I am his. During some seasons, he made sacrifices to support me and my endeavors; in other ones, I made sacrifices to support his. For instance, when I wrote my first book, *The Fringe Hours: Making Time for You*, I did the bulk of my writing on weekends, while Matthew handled the bulk of the home and parenting responsibilities. The same was true during the writing of this book. When Matthew had the opportunity to travel around the world for a month on a writing and photography gig with a major media company, I didn't blink an eye in supporting him in that. Were those times hard? Sure. But they were also rewarding personally and professionally for each of us. Having the opportunity to cheer each other on is a great joy in our marriage.

In addition to the times we have served each other, however, we have had times when we did not see eye to eye and marriage was a struggle. During those seasons, we had to work harder to be connected and intimate. And I'm not talking about sex here. Intimacy is about much more than physical touch. The following list of types of intimacy shows how many ways couples can connect with each other:

- sexual intimacy: sharing passion and physical pleasuring
- emotional intimacy: being tuned to each other's wavelength
- intellectual intimacy: closeness in the world of ideas
- aesthetic intimacy: sharing experience of beauty
- creative intimacy: sharing in acts of creating together
- recreational intimacy: relating in experiences of fun and play
- work intimacy: closeness in sharing common tasks
- crisis intimacy: closeness in coping with problems and pain

- conflict intimacy: facing and struggling with differences
- commitment intimacy: mutually derived from common self-interest
- spiritual intimacy: unity shared in religious expression
- communication intimacy: mutual understanding and affirmation
- moral intimacy: shared sense of what is right[1]

In which of these areas do you and your significant other experience intimacy? Which types of intimacy occur regularly, and which types could use some cultivating? Were certain types of intimacy new to you? When I was introduced to this list, I was immediately struck by "work intimacy" and recognized how much shared work means to me. For example, in our house, I tend to do most of the laundry. One day last week I came home to a stack of folded sheets that Matthew had taken care of while I was at work. I was caught off guard by how happy this simple act made me. I shared the experience and my happiness with Dr. Kristie Overstreet, a clinical sexologist, who affirmed my reaction, saying, "Doesn't that kind of make a part of you say, 'Oh, that's wonderful!' And then, even if it's a little bit subconscious, next time he needs you to do something, or asks, you're right there probably doing it. And you kind of think, 'Well, hey, he helped me do this, so I'm going to help him do that.' And that's how you collaborate and really help meet each other's needs."[2]

That simple stack of folded sheets is an excellent example of just one of the types of intimacy we need to share. Ultimately, all the different types of intimacy play a role in the health of our relationship, the tenderness we feel toward each other, and our emotions. Tending to each of them as well as recognizing where we fall short and working on those areas will strengthen our relationship.

For parents who work, feelings of being stretched too thin can make connecting harder. And in many houses, both parents are working. According to the Bureau of Labor Statistics, "Among families with children, 89.3 percent had at least one employed parent in 2015. Among married-couple families with children, 96.7 percent had at least one employed parent; both parents worked in 60.6 percent of married-couple families."[3] If you fall into this last category and feel your marriage is not getting your best, consider the following tips for ways to strengthen your relationship. These are all things we know instinctually but might need to be reminded of for our day-to-day relationship.

Communicate Well

My husband, Matthew, and I met in 2003 via the now defunct AOL instant messenger. Yep, we met on the internet before that was really a thing. He was the editor of a Christian music magazine called *CCM*. I was a junior in college at the University of Wisconsin–Madison and had plans to spend the summer in Nashville interning for a major Christian record label. I had an issue of the magazine in my dorm room to gain knowledge about the industry.

As editors do, Matthew had published a monthly "Letter from the Editor" column, along with an AOL instant messenger name. After reading his piece, I added "CCMeditor" to my AOL friends list, not knowing how that action would change my life.

One night Matthew was online, and I instant messaged him, inquiring about the music industry and the magazine. Almost instantly, no pun intended, we clicked in a way that was very different from how we had connected with anyone either of us had ever met. Within a week, he gave me his number, and we began talking on the phone. Over the course of the next five months, we talked every day, usually for hours. This was before the days of Facetime, and Skype was not even universal (neither of us had cameras for our computers anyway). We simply relied on our words to get to know each other.

During those months, we learned each other's stories. We shared everything over those long, late-night phone calls—our family histories, our work, our dreams, our favorite things. We laughed. We cried. We invested hours and hours truly getting to know each other. All of our sharing laid a strong foundation for when we would finally meet in person—and by that time we were in love.

Yes, it sounds very *You've Got Mail*, and in a way, it was. Matthew and I had an undeniable heart connection from the very beginning of our relationship. It was deep, made rich by the hours we had invested in really getting to know each other.

Our stories play a huge role in our relationships, and continually investing in learning about the other person is important. Oftentimes when a couple is not connecting, the problem can be linked to their needing what clinical director Bill Lokey of Onsite workshops calls a "heart connection." He advises couples to take the time to eliminate distractions and simply sit together and talk, enabling them to reconnect in a meaningful way. He shared with me a few of the ways he encourages couples to reconnect:

- *Share a high and a low of the day.* Opening up about the best and the worst parts of your day presents an opportunity for encouragement and love. This also will likely be a chance to talk about work in an open and honest manner.
- *Read together.* Choose a book you will both enjoy, and end the day reading to each other. Just as reading to your kids provides quality time, the same will happen for you and your spouse. Don't get caught up in the genre of the book—whatever is appealing will suffice. The nurturing atmosphere of reading aloud paves the way for connection with your spouse.

    Working mom Anna shared that she and her husband read together on vacation.

When we're away, he will read out loud while we're in bed. The intimacy of sharing written words and a story in your head can be very special. Watching someone speak, hearing their voice, and even feeling their breath are things we don't tend to do naturally. When they read to you, you automatically watch their mouth and tongue move around the words and their facial expressions change. Lines in their skin appear then disappear. Muscles in the cheeks, jaw, chin, and brow tighten, stretch, and relax. You really hear their voice as you listen to the story. You hear them take a breath and take a quick sniff from their nose as they resync their breathing pattern. If you're near enough, you may feel the heat of their exhale on your ear, neck, or face. In bed I've smelled the toothpaste on my husband's breath as he speaks. Even a faint aroma of garlic and alcohol can be comforting in such an intimate shared moment. Your own breathing begins to sync with theirs as you become aware of the rhythm of their chest, as they breathe in to catch the next word. For me, it's made me want to place my hand on his chest as it moves up and down, inhaling and exhaling characters, plots, and chapters.[4]

- *Play a board game.* Board games are a simple but effective way to connect. When Matthew and I were newlyweds, we used to play Scrabble regularly. But as our careers took off and our family grew, the game gathered dust at the top of a closet. We have recently begun playing games together again, and the simple act of playing a game has helped us turn off devices at night and connect with each other.

- *Ask each other a starter question.* Certain questions are designed to unpack a person's personal narrative. While they might seem silly initially, they are great prompts for genuine connection. A few ideas are:

What is your favorite memory from your childhood?
What is a memory you have about your mom?

What is your favorite game and why?

What is the most embarrassing experience of your life?

Who do you admire most in your life, and why do you admire this person?

- *End the day with a prayer*. Another opportunity to connect can come through praying together. By presenting your prayers and petitions to God as one marital unit, you will forge a stronger connection.[5]

Communicating well with your spouse is critical to having a healthy relationship. You have to be vulnerable and honest. Share what is going on in your life, where you need help, and how you are feeling. Don't expect your spouse to be a mind reader. Nearly every major argument Matthew and I have had was born out of a lack of communication. One of us would get to the point where we were so frustrated that we exploded. Looking back on those times, had one of us spoken up sooner, much of that anger and frustration could have been avoided.

Practice Active Listening

Listening goes hand in hand with communication. Active listening, when your spouse truly has your attention, ensures that you are both really heard, that negativity doesn't occur, and that your relationship is strengthened.

When having a conversation, face each other and look into each other's eyes. If I'm not sure my husband is listening to me, I will say, "Can you please look at me so I know you are listening?" This helps center both of us for speaking and listening actively. If a conversation starts across rooms or while one of us is doing something, such as helping one of our kids or cooking dinner, one of us will usually move to be near the other. Moving to the same room guarantees that nothing is missed and that our conversation is given the attention it deserves.

Also, don't listen with an ear for how you are going to respond or interrupt with questions or reactions. Instead, completely focus your attention on listening to your spouse. When he is done speaking, that is the time to respond appropriately. This can be a tough one for me, as my mind often goes immediately to questions or solutions. But I have learned that if I interject, Matthew can feel he is not being heard. This feeling can lead to frustration and resentment, which are not healthy in a marriage. Asking questions can also take the conversation in a different direction than what the speaker intends, so be careful with questions and stick to the topic at hand.

Also, be sure to listen with both head and heart. If a conversation is difficult, resist the urge to become reactionary. Instead, listen with patience and respond with humility. Hopefully, your spouse will do the same for you.

Trust Your Spouse

Often when we talk about trust in relationship to marriage, it is in regard to sexual faithfulness. But trust is about so much more than this. It's also about having confidence that what your spouse says is true.

When my husband says, "I want you to go out with your friends and have fun," I must trust that he means what he says. Yet I can easily let doubt slip in and question things—Does he really want me to go? Can he handle things? Does he resent my schedule?—when, in fact, nothing he said should make me think this way. Don't let your insecurities impact the trust you have in your spouse and his words.

You must also trust that your spouse is not going to reject you or abandon you when disagreements happen. Your spouse is your closest friend and confidant. He wants what is best for you, just as you do for him. Don't let fear prevent you from being transparent about your feelings and desires. Sometimes disagreements will and do happen, but knowing in your core that no disagreement will break your union creates a spirit of safety in your relationship. You will be able to be more vulnerable and honest when you can rely on this deep trust of each other.

Spend Quality Time Together

When our schedules get hectic, the first thing we edit from our day is often time with the one we love the most. If that happens once in a while, that's okay. But you don't want to let it become the routine. Counselor Dawn Sturkey shared this wisdom with me: "The routine becomes the boss."[6] We typically think of routine or structure in regard to our family or our work, but applying the same principle to marriage is helpful. You want your routine with your spouse to include intimate connection and quality time.

Carving out quality time with your spouse can be difficult, especially if you both work and are juggling kid responsibilities. But fight for that time. Dawn recommends to many of the couples she counsels that Sunday night is typically a good night to spend time together. Most people don't work on Sundays, and kids often will go to bed earlier than on a Friday or Saturday night.[7] While planning "this is our time" might sound unromantic, having this standing us time has proved to be effective in my own marriage. Sunday night is definitely our time. The kids know that Mommy and Daddy watch a show together on Sunday night and that they need to be in bed promptly at bedtime. We turn down the lights, snuggle on the couch, and enjoy the quiet and being together.

Matthew and I also make sure we get out once in a while for a bit more extended quality time. Some couples schedule a standing date night and book a babysitter months in advance. When I was in high school, I babysat for a teacher and her spouse once a month. I didn't realize then how much that simple tradition would stick with me into adulthood. Though they were busy with young twins, they still made getting out of the house and having alone time a priority.

If I know a particularly busy season is coming, I will often buy tickets to a show as a way to ensure that Matthew and I will get a night out. (Living in Nashville, we are spoiled with lots of opportunities to see live music and performances!) Even though the timing sometimes feels overwhelming, we never regret having that one-on-one time together. Right before our daughter, Adeline, was born, we went to the local symphony to see Idina Menzel (of *Rent* and *Frozen* fame), and it was incredible. Thankfully, I didn't go into labor, though the people around us were nervous! That night out was a special memory for us before we became a family of four.

When you spend time with your spouse, try not to talk about the kids. Instead, focus on each other, your dreams, hopes, and goals. Speak words of love to each other. Hold hands and enjoy the time away. Be intentional about pursuing that needed time together.

Practice Physical Intimacy

We have spent a lot of time unpacking the importance of good communication and strong connections, which are the building blocks for positive physical intimacy. Sex is an important part of a healthy relationship. When we are emotionally connected, says Bill Lokey, physical arousal is more likely to happen. "We are most attractive to our partner when we are doing whatever that thing is that has us in our sweet spot."[8] My husband has commented many times that there is nothing sexier than when he sees me speaking to an audience, teaching on a topic in my wheelhouse. Now, I'm not saying that I finish speaking and we have sex! But the idea that being our truest selves and leaning into our callings is attractive is so encouraging, isn't it?

Be committed to making time for physical intimacy. I've heard it said that while sex isn't the most important aspect of a marital relationship, when it's not happening, it quickly becomes the most important part of the relationship. That's why it's important not to push sexual intimacy aside for extended periods of time because of exhaustion or busyness. That physicality brings about deep connectedness in your relationship.

Also, recognize what your physical needs are and share them with your husband. Yes, this may be awkward to talk about, but sharing what brings you pleasure with your spouse will lead to better, deeper physical and emotional intimacy.

Show Kindness and Be Polite

Sometimes we let our manners relax with those closest to us. I can be so sweet to clients and colleagues and then nasty with my husband. That's awful! This should go without saying, but be cognizant of the way you treat your spouse. Strive to be loving, kind, and polite. Use words such as *please* and *thank you*, and use them often and intentionally. As Proverbs says, "Kind words are like honey—sweet to the soul and healthy for the body" (16:24 NLT).

The way you treat your spouse will have an impact on how your family members interact with one another and how you engage with other people. Be mindful of the example you are setting for your children, knowing that the way you treat your spouse will influence the way they treat their spouses someday.

Consider practicing random acts of kindness in your home. Surprise your spouse with a written note of affirmation. In an age when texts and emails are the norm, a handwritten card or note is a simple way to show you care. I keep a small stack of "I love you" postcards and periodically write on the back of one and slip it in my husband's laptop case. The note is a nice surprise for him when he opens up his case to start his work for the day. Kindness always is appreciated, and the ones we love the most should experience it the most frequently.

Ask for Help

This point goes back to the one about good communication, but it bears repeating. If you need help, ask your spouse for it. Sometimes you might need to repeat your request or change your expectations, but none of that can happen if you don't ask the first time. Your spouse is not a mind reader. By being vulnerable enough to say, "I need help with XYZ," you empower your spouse to step in and you empower yourself by verbalizing your needs. Instead of taking on too much or expecting too little and becoming overwhelmed, ask for help.

Over the years, I have learned again and again that so much frustration and resentment is rooted in one of us not speaking up and saying what we need. When I am forthright about my needs, my husband is quick to take action and step in or to help figure out a solution to the problem.

Earlier in this book, we talked about the mental load that women carry. Much of your mental load can be relieved by having honest though sometimes difficult conversations with your spouse and asking for help with things at home.

For instance, during a season when I had to work a lot of overtime, I found it difficult to keep up with the laundry. My husband is great at many things, but laundry is not his strong suit. So after I waved the white flag and said I needed help, we decided together to get someone to come in and help take care of laundry during this busy season.

Asking for help makes us feel vulnerable because we are admitting we can't do it all. (This is healthy and normal—no one can do it all!) But it also sometimes causes disagreements, which is why women often avoid asking in the first place. If this is true in your relationship, don't let fear of confrontation prevent you from bringing up an area of struggle. Hard conversations can result in positive change.

Overcome Resentment

Resentment is not something that happens overnight. It is usually a slow build. And often the resentment we feel is caused by another emotion. When couples enter therapy with Dr. Kristie Overstreet, she often gives them homework related to resentment, saying that "resentment is anger that's turned inward." She typically has couples make three lists about the three major types of resentment, citing that "it can feel overwhelming to think of all the anger and resentment we may have. When people separate them out, they find that there's maybe not quite as many as they thought. And separating them out helps them see which ones they need to work on the most." Consider the following types of resentment, and evaluate which, if any, you are harboring and what you need to do to overcome them.

> *Resentment toward self.* Consider the resentments that are directed inward, such as anger, frustration, comparison (all the things we addressed earlier in the book).
>
> *Resentment toward spouse.* Consider negative feelings you are harboring that are specific to your spouse. These might be related to specific habits, an incident, finances, or something else.
>
> *General resentment.* Consider what other areas you might be feeling resentment in, such as work, challenges with friends, etc.

Kristie shared that once couples are able to see where their resentments are coming from, they can then do the hard work of resolving those issues.[9]

Don't Blame

The blame game does nothing but fuel resentment and frustration, causing hurt in ourselves. Instead of blaming your spouse, consider the role you played in a situation. Ask yourself, "How can I make this better? What changes do I need to make?" This introspective exercise can be very revealing and will transform both your heart and the situation. Oftentimes when you are able to see yourself and make changes, doing so helps propel a situation forward. Don't be afraid to share openly and honestly what you are feeling and working on so that both you and your spouse can move forward in a healthy manner.

Practice Forgiveness

The most freeing thing you can do in your relationship is practice forgiveness often and quickly. The sooner you forgive, the happier you both will be. By truly forgiving, you will not be held hostage by anger, jealousy, frustration, and pain. Harboring these emotions will only ruin you and your marriage. Forgiveness doesn't mean you condone a behavior. You can and should still share how something made you feel and the hurt you may have experienced while also moving forward.

Matthew and I wrote our own vows when we got married. In them, we promised never to go to bed angry. By never ending a day without forgiveness, we are so much happier. I didn't realize then the profoundly positive impact this would have on our marriage for years to come. If you've never made a similar promise to your spouse, I encourage you to do so now.

Have Grace

At the end of the day, you and your spouse love your family and each other. Lavishly show grace toward each other. Mistakes happen. Miscommunication happens. Things sometimes work out differently than you anticipated. I can't count the number of times I have apologized to Matthew and he has extended grace to me. It is one of the most beautiful gifts you can give your spouse. Marriage and relationships take real work. It is hard work, but all good things require hard work.

I'll never forget when I was newly married and a colleague and I were traveling together. She had been married for about ten years. Over dinner she shared with me how remarkable it was that after about ten years of marriage, many of her friends were divorcing. She said, "Just wait—you'll see the same thing happen." Sure enough, Matthew and I have been married fourteen years, and we have seen many friends recently get divorced. It has broken our hearts. Another colleague and I were discussing this same trend. She has been married for twenty-five years, and she said, "You'll see it again when your kids are grown. I was at a party recently, and 50 percent of the women there were divorced. For many couples, after their kids leave the house, they realize they have nothing left. They don't even know each other."

These stories are reminders of the ongoing care and constant attention marriages need to thrive. They can't be set on cruise control for years. Yes, divorce happens for many reasons, and I am not saying that neglect is always one of them. But I am saying that it is important to focus on each other, love well, communicate with intention, and celebrate each other's successes, even when life is busy at work and with kids.

The words "'til death do us part" signify a bond that will outlast your job, the years your children spend at home, and basically everything else you hold close. Love your spouse well, and cultivate a deeply rooted marriage.

Reflections on Your Marriage

On a scale of 1 to 10, how happy are you in your marriage?

(1) (2) (3) (4) (5) (6) (7) (8) (9) (10)

not happy　　　　　　**sort of happy**　　　　　**very happy**

Using that same scale, how do you think your spouse would answer that question? Perhaps invite them to answer.

_____

_____

_____

_____

If you're not happy, why do you think that is? While only you a
your spouse can know for sure what might be causing distan
in your relationship, don't be afraid to consider seeking help
counseling from a professional marriage therapist. There's
shame in asking for help when trying to navigate any emot
or challenges you and your significant other might be facir

_____

_____

_____

_____

Plan a date night. It doesn't have to be fancy or expensive. If possible, plan something that involves going out because leaving your home eliminates distractions. Record what you are going to do below.

Having conversations with your spouse about your long-term dreams and goals is important. Have you shared these aspirations with your spouse? If not, take time to do so this week and record how it went below.

Are you feeling resentful? If so, write down if it is resentment toward self, toward your spouse, or general resentment, as well as why. Then find an opportunity this week to have an honest conversation so that this feeling (or feelings) won't take root in your life.

In what area could you use some help from your spouse? Write it down, along with a commitment to discuss it. _____

Write a love letter to your spouse or significant other. Not an email or a text. An actual handwritten note. Say what you love about him, how he makes you feel, why he's your best friend. Leave the note where it will surprise him when you are not around—in the bathroom, on his driver's seat, in his lunch.

SEVEN

Parenting Well

As we begin this chapter, first and foremost, know this: you are a great mom. The very fact that you are reading this book tells me so. Don't beat yourself up. Parenting is a hard job, and it's a journey. As cliché as this sounds, it isn't a destination. We are constantly evolving in our parenting, just as we are growing and changing in every area of our lives.

I'll never forget when my little girl said to me, "Mama, I don't want you to go to work. I want you to be with me forever."

I knelt down beside her and hugged her close. As I stroked her hair, I said, "Oh, baby girl, I love you so much, but Mommy has to work. Working allows Mommy to use the talents God has given her as well as help provide things like food for our family and toys for you, Elias, and Ezra."

She nodded her head and said, "Like I'm going to be a singer someday because God made me a good singer?"

"Yep, just like that. And even though you will be writing songs and singing for people, you will still love your kids with all your heart, just like I love you."

I always knew I would be a working mom. My mom worked, as did her mother before her. While I have been struck by all the feelings over the years—mom guilt, comparison, questioning whether it is worth it—I have always come back to yes, this is what I am supposed to do. My work has value. My calling doesn't mean I can't also be an incredible mother, and the same is true for you. If you are feeling stretched too thin as a parent, consider the following ways you can connect with your kids, no matter their age, and foster meaningful time together.

Connecting with Your Kids

I don't want to look back on my children's lives and think, *Wow, we spent so much time "doing" that we were hardly living.* I also don't want to feel like I worked so much that I was parenting from a place of emptiness, which is why self-care is so important, as we discussed in chapter 4.

In Renee Peterson Trudeau's excellent book, *Nurturing the Soul of Your Family: 10 Ways to Reconnect and Find Peace in Everyday Life,* she writes in the introduction, "There is no greater spiritual work than conscious parenting and agreeing to live with other beings on this level of intimacy. More than anything, we all crave connection and community. This starts at home and it starts right now—not a month or a year from now. Now is the time to awaken, heal, open our hearts and reconnect with the most important people we'll ever know."[1]

I love how Renee calls us to act right now. In our busyness, we can easily put things off. Sometimes it seems as if the more important something is, the bigger it feels and the more likely we will put it off. Don't settle for the status quo. Just because you work and have many responsibilities doesn't mean that passively settling into a routine is the right approach. You might need to shake things up in order to cultivate meaningful experiences with your kids that will positively impact them for a lifetime.

Routine Times to Connect

I have a print hanging on my bulletin board at work featuring a Jill Churchill quote that says, "There's no way to be a perfect mother and a million ways to be a good one."

While I can't give you that list of one million ways, I can provide some ideas for connecting with your children during certain times of the day. You'll notice that these are times you already spend with your children. I'm not recommending a radical shift in when you spend time with your children but rather intention in how you spend that time. Instead of frantic hustle, choose to be fully present. Later in this chapter, we will go over some other habits you can incorporate into your family's journey that may help fuel connections with one another.

Much of a child's day is focused on academics and extracurriculars. Use the opportunities you have to be with your children to connect emotionally and spiritually. Focus on quality time together, which will look different based on the season and ages of your kids. Think about the following times you have together.

■ Morning

Mornings offer an excellent way to start your day with your children on a positive note. During the week, many parents look at mornings with the end goal in mind—get out the door. But consider those precious first few hours as an opportunity for quality time with your children. Eat breakfast together, read together, or go through your child's schoolwork together, commenting on what you like and discussing what they're learning. If you work evening hours, you might find that while you can't always be home for evening mealtimes, you can have the same quality conversations with your kids around the breakfast table. If you have an early riser, you might be able to do a physical activity together, such as going for a quick run or doing yoga. A teen daughter might enjoy doing her makeup with you, and that time together can be an opportunity for meaningful conversation.

Cultivating connection opportunities in the morning might mean you need to get up earlier and/or prepare the night before to ensure you can have this quality time together. But these small sacrifices can have a significant impact on your children, both in the short term, as they leave for school feeling loved, and in the long term, as they look back on their childhood.

I love having mornings with my children that involve doing something together before school and work. Of course, this doesn't happen every morning, but on the mornings that it does, I leave for work feeling more settled in my spirit and joyful in my heart. I also believe that my kids go to school feeling extra cared for, even though they are too young to articulate those feelings.

■ Lunch

This midday fuel break can be an opportunity to connect with your children, particularly if they are elementary aged. Many schools invite parents to join their children for lunch. While my work schedule doesn't permit me to do this often, I try to schedule it a few times a year. Those lunches are always so special. If you have a high-school-aged child, they may be permitted to leave campus for lunch. If so, ask if they would want to have lunch with you. Use the time to connect with your child one-on-one in an atypical setting.

If having lunch together isn't an option, think of another way to show affection. Maybe slip a note in your child's lunch box or include their favorite treat for dessert. My mom would always make holidays special when packing our lunches. I remember her making an all green lunch on St. Patrick's Day, complete with a green drink, a shamrock cookie, and green swirled bread (which I didn't eat because I thought it looked too much like mold!). As a child, I thought my mom was just being funny, but now I recognize her intention and thoughtfulness in putting those lunches together even while she was busy managing our home and work responsibilities.

For older children, make a note of when their lunch break is and send them a text to let them know you are thinking of them. This loving gesture might be just the thing they need to get through a long day at school—and help you while at work too!

■ Car Rides

Throughout the day, car rides can be an opportunity to connect with your kids. For my first six years as a parent, I did the majority of the day care drop-offs and pickups. This was sixty minutes I had in the car with my kids each day. We would talk about their day, sing songs, pray, and just enjoy one another's company. No matter how difficult my day was at work, this time together started and ended my workday on a memorable note. I will always treasure those times together.

My friends with older kids tell me that car time continues to be an opportunity for great connections, though the conversations shift from ABCs to relationships, school challenges, and more. Make a point to look at times in the car with your children not as a burden of going from point A to point B but as a gift to have uninterrupted time to talk.

■ Evenings

Evenings are a key time for working moms to connect with their children. While extracurricular activities, schoolwork, and dinner might take center stage, still allow for some time to connect. Ask your children about their day, their friends, and anything they might be struggling with. Be open and accessible, not impatient and rushed. By keeping your focus on their words, body language, and so on, you can be a more engaged parent.

While children thrive on routine, spontaneous fun is always welcome too. For instance, we have a neighborhood pool. While many families are there during the day in the summer months, that isn't feasible for us because Matthew and I both work. I always enjoy watching the reaction when I proclaim after dinner, "Let's go to the pool!" The kids shriek with delight and run to get their swimming suits on. We always have a great time together. And yes, on those nights all the dishes might not get done, but that's okay. The memories made are so much more important.

For older kids, evenings are typically the times they want to open up and have more serious, honest conversations. My friend Kristin has three teenagers, and she shared with me the importance of being available when kids are wanting to talk, even if it is late and you're ready for bed. "If we can just be patient and not let our tired emotions get the best of us, we create a safe place for them to share their worries and fears. We let them know that no subject is off-limits. This requires me practicing a bit of a poker face when heavier topics come up! My husband and I want our kids to feel comfortable coming to us in the hard times of their lives instead of to a friend who might not steer them in a healthy direction."[2]

■ Bedtime

Bedtime is also a critical time to connect with your children, especially when they are young. There's something about the quietness of a dark room that encourages children to open up or be extra affectionate. My kids love to ask me questions, talk about their day, and smother me with kisses at bedtime. Some nights I'm tired from the go, go, go of the day, and if I'm really honest, I want to skip the bedtime shenanigans—because of course plenty of nights also involve requests for water and one last trip to the bathroom. But I'm always glad when I say, "Yes, Mommy will put you to bed." I know these days won't last, so I work to be intentional and treasure them.

■ Weekends

If you have a traditional work schedule, you are likely off on weekends. If you are self-employed or work untraditional hours, this may not be the case. Regardless, school-aged children are home on the weekend, so it is important to think about how the weekend can be used to invest in your children and your relationship with them.

Plan quality time together. If you have more than one child, try to plan one-on-one times. The activity might be as simple as going for a walk around the block or going to get an ice-cream cone. Our family typically has a healthy mix of fun and chores on weekends. I am always grateful for two solid days together.

As you consider these various chunks of time, think about what your family enjoys doing together. Is it playing games? Going for walks? Being in the kitchen? Whatever it is, use such activities to connect during everyday life.

Other Connection Points

In addition to utilizing various chunks of time in the typical day and week, think about other opportunities for connection with your children. Keep in mind that, for older kids, planning time with them is helpful, as they tend to have fuller schedules due to extracurricular activities, social engagements, and job commitments. If you feel it is important for your child to be a part of something, such as a family dinner or an outing, be sure to communicate that expectation. Kindly ask them to add the event to their calendar so it is made a priority. Giving your child advance notice and clear expectations is useful and shows attentiveness.

▪ Family Meetings

Family meetings can be a helpful way to connect and ensure that everyone is on the same page. Meetings can be formal or informal, but they should have the goal of informing everyone of schedules, rules, and other family matters. Faith Cracraft, academic advisor and mom to a little girl, shared:

> Right now family meetings are just me and my husband. With our scheduling demands—him being in school, two full-time jobs outside the home (one day shift, one night shift), volunteer roles, and a side passion gig, we have an in-depth review of our calendar and budget monthly with a weekly check-in. We try to value Sabbath, so we literally shade out one weekend day a week where there are no major plans scheduled. It's so helpful to be on the same page when working different schedules with lots of demands.[3]

Melissa Wooten is a single mom to two sons (ages twenty-nine and seventeen) and has found family meetings to be critically important with her son who is still at home, saying, "We have a family meeting every Sunday after dinner. We discuss schedules, the week's menu, any supply or items needed for the week. The last Sunday of the month we discuss any special things we want to do the next month and get it on the calendar. Doing this weekly has helped us have open communication and make sure we make time for the important things."[4]

▪ Family Dinners

Meals are a natural opportunity for connection. When my husband and I first got married, we tended to eat in the living room because we had a very tiny dining space. This habit carried over to our new house, even though it has a dining room. As our family grew and our children got older, I recognized that we were missing out on an opportunity to communicate well with one another. Instead, our eyes were glued on the television, wondering if a chef was going to beat Bobby Flay. So we shifted and starting having more dinners in our dining room. The kids help set the table, and we enjoy talking with one another. We have everyone share three highlights from their day as well as one thing that was tough. This has become my favorite part of the day, and our relationships have all been strengthened because of this time around the table.

Ann Voskamp's family reads the Bible together after every meal. A mom of seven and a bestselling author, Ann is very intentional about her time with her children. This practice of reading started when her husband was a child, and it is one they adopted in parenting their children. She said:

> I can honestly say the very best thing I've ever done is open up Scripture at the end of every meal and read together. Sometimes we wrestle through hard things, whether it's in the headlines or culture or their own challenges. Of all the things we've done, it centers us and allows us to say there's always room at the table for your questions, for you to be real, and there's always real living bread for you at the table that will sustain your soul.[5]

Angela, a corporate communications executive and mom of two, also finds many meaningful ways to connect with her kids over meals. She says:

> My husband and I often use dinnertimes to broaden our understanding of the world and will often discuss current events with our two teens. Also, at least once a month, we try to make a new dish from another country. For instance, every March we usually do something Irish, around Easter we will make something traditionally Jewish, one night we even made a traditional Indian dish and watched *Bend It Like Beckham* together. This has become even more fun since we all became vegetarians. Dinners for us look very casual and full of witty banter over subjects like politics, religion, marketing campaigns, college and career talk, and typical teenage happenings like school dances, classes, and sporting events.[6]

▪ Vacations

Have you ever heard the saying "A vacation with kids is just parenting in a different location"? This makes me smile because, yes, vacationing with my three kids is far different than going to Mexico with my girlfriends. However, when I look back on our family's vacation memories, whether they were simple day trips or weeklong trips to the beach, the first word that comes to mind is *precious*. Vacations give everyone a chance to explore, experience wonder, and unwind a bit from the daily grind of regular life. When kids get older, vacations also offer an opportunity for everyone to get involved in the planning. As a working mom, I enjoy vacations because they give me a chance to focus more on my family.

▪ Weekly Traditions

Our family is very intentional about weekly traditions. Typically, Thursday is game night, and Friday is movie night. Our kids look forward to picking a movie that we can all watch as a family. We used to pick out the movie on Friday night, but now we select it earlier in the week, which eliminates bickering and adds to the excitement for what is to come. We eat dinner and then snuggle on the couch with blankets. Sometimes I will lie down on the couch and have room to snuggle with just one child. Usually, the big kids insist on switching off so they both get a turn with my arms around them. I know these years are fleeting, and I love breathing in the sweet smell of their hair and feeling the rise and fall of their chests. Those times together will be some of my dearest memories of their childhoods.

My friend Lysa and her family have Monday night family dinners. These nights have always had an open-door policy, allowing her kids to invite friends over to enjoy great food and great conversation. By starting this tradition, Lysa created memories with her family, connection with her kids, and good relationships with their friends.[7]

■ Birthdays

I grew up in a home in which birthdays were a big deal. I would go to bed and wake up in the morning to find balloons taped on my door and crepe paper strewn across the kitchen. My dad would make my bed, and my mom would make a dinner of my choice. They didn't let their work get in the way of making my sister and me feel appreciated. Now as a mother, I try to make birthdays magical for our kids too, usually by making a special meal, singing to them, and throwing a party.

Working mom Amy has teenagers and works forty miles from her kids' school, which means they need to ride the bus to and from school. She shared, "On their birthdays, I schedule an afternoon off from work so I can pick them up from school and they get to bypass the dreaded school bus, at least for an afternoon. They always look forward to me picking them up on their birthday. It also allows me to cook a nice meal of their choice."[8]

Birthdays are the perfect opportunity to celebrate your children, and they will surely look back on those days with fondness. Be thoughtful about how you can do a little extra to show love to your child on their birthday. No matter their age—this thoughtfulness will be treasured.

■ While Practicing Gratitude

Practicing gratitude as a family is not something that should be limited to Thanksgiving. Instead, find a way to show gratefulness all year long. For our family, I bought a spiral calendar that sits in our dining room. Each day each family member is responsible to write one thing they are thankful for. The calendar is easy to store and very accessible. I love that this act provides writing practice for my children and is capturing their handwriting at this age. I know we will look back through those calendars in the years to come, and they will be deeply treasured. Other families hang a gratitude poster for people to write on or use white boards to write a daily thankfulness message.

Take time to let your kids know you are grateful for them, and be specific about your reasons why. When our eldest is kind to his younger siblings, we make a point to tell him that we are grateful for his kind and patient spirit toward them. Positive affirmation and gratitude build our kids up and are things they will carry with them far beyond the actual conversation.

Be generous with your gratitude. The method isn't important, but the act is. Practicing gratitude leads to happier people, and happy people lead to happy families!

■ While Traveling

If your work requires you to travel, use your time away as an opportunity to be intentional about showing love to your children. Leave them notes in their backpacks or lunch boxes. If they are older, text them to let them know you are thinking about them. Facetime with them before school. Bring home a small gift to show them they were remembered. The what isn't as important as the actual demonstration of love.

■ Homecomings

I love this idea from working mom Jennie Evans. When a family member has been away for several days (i.e., at camp), the family celebrates their return home. Jennie always makes sure their room is clean and the bed has fresh sheets on it. The entire family partakes in a special meal (child's choice, which they share in advance of leaving) and hears all about the child's experience.[9]

The fact that you are a working mom doesn't mean you are a "less than" parent, but it does mean you may need to use creativity to ensure that you are investing instead of surviving in your relationships with your children. By considering the regular times of your day or week and both planned and spontaneous moments that you have to spend with your children, you can be proactive in your choices to listen, speak truth, and love well.

Be a Mom Who Is . . .

No matter what kind of work we do or the number of hours we invest in our career, the way we treat our children and how we act matter. I want to be a mom who loves my children well, teaches them practical tools and important life lessons, and is present when I'm with them. The following attributes and actions are a lens you can use for considering how you parent.

Be a Mom Who Is Self-Aware

As you pursue parenting with intention, you need to be self-aware. Dr. Fran Walfish, Beverly Hills family and relationship psychotherapist and author of *The Self-Aware Parent*, said, "To be a self-aware parent is to always be curious about yourself and your own behavior and to be open enough to be willing to look within and to be accountable." She went on to add, "Accountability is crucial to all relationships, including parenting. Some of us think that you cannot say you made a mistake or say you're sorry to your child or you'll lose respect, and in fact the opposite is true. That's how you gain your child's greater respect."[10]

I know that self-awareness has played a crucial role in the way I parent. When I am agitated, stressed, or overwhelmed by work, those emotions sometimes impact the way I speak to my children. I have seen the way their whole demeanor changes when I fly off the handle for something insignificant.

One morning during a particularly intense workweek, our cleaning service was coming at 8:00 a.m. In addition to getting ready for school, the kids needed to help straighten up the house for the crew. We had the TV on for our two-year-old so the rest of us could work. Despite repeatedly being asked to help, our eldest son kept getting distracted by the television. I lost it, yelling so loudly and angrily that he jumped. It was not a good moment for me.

After stepping away for a few minutes, I went back to him and asked for his forgiveness. He hugged me around my waist and forgave me with a smile. On the way to work, I called my husband, asking his forgiveness for my actions, explaining how much work was getting to me. He gently said that all was forgiven and that he knew the pressure I was under.

Had I not been self-aware, my behavior could have negatively impacted everyone's day. By quickly recognizing that I was wrong and apologizing, I was able to turn things around and model better behavior. To be sure, sometimes I still need to be called out—we all do! I'm grateful that my husband will let me know when the way I am parenting isn't the best, and he expects the same of me.

Lynn Zakeri, LCSW, Chicago-area therapist, affirms that the situation I described above is one that many working moms have gone through, and it definitely impacts our kids. She shared, "Kids become afraid of judgment. When you're working and stressed out, there's a need of passing on perfectionism. There's no time for mistakes. There's no time for silliness. They think about what Mom is 'gonna do,' such as Mom is going to be really mad if the house is a mess." She went on to add, "I tell my kids all the time the maddest I get at them is when I'm stressed out, so they have to call me out and say, 'Why are you yelling?' Then I can take a step back and say, 'You're right. It's because I am thinking about this thing I have to do for work, and it's not you guys, it's me.' They feel better because there's understanding both ways, and we can move on from it."[11]

By making the conscious effort to be a self-aware parent, you become in tune with the way your circumstances and moods impact your family. You are then able to make better choices regarding the words you say and the actions you take. Furthermore, you can encourage your children to join you in the process of becoming more self-aware by asking them to call you out when you are acting out due to stress.

Be a Mom Who Is Relaxed

Calm down. Being tightly wound and stressed does not help anyone. Don't let things get the best of you and then take out your frustrations on your kids. Instead, slow down and relax in your parenting. Take things as they come.

I noticed I was often getting stressed out with my kids on school mornings. I felt I was constantly harping on them about tasks to be accomplished (Eat your breakfast! Get dressed! Brush your teeth!), and I was making mornings terrible. I decided to buy a chart from the Dollar Tree and write all their morning tasks on it. This simple chart was a morning game changer. They could easily assess what they needed to do every morning, I stopped yelling and relaxed, and the dynamic of our mornings was more positive.

My friend Shane is a self-employed mom of three teens and shared this wise advice with me: "I think it is important to be yourself in how you engage with your kids. Don't be afraid to be silly or weird, and be willing to talk about sex and culture in everyday conversation. Sometimes I take myself as a parent so seriously, and it's helped to relax and laugh when they are talking about things they hear, body parts, etc. and not always worry about constantly teaching them."[12]

Be a Mom Who Is Honest

Don't shy away from telling the truth to your children. Honesty is the best policy—always. If you have a busy season at work, explain to them what you are doing and when you will be home, and state that you know it is a hard season. While writing this book, I often left our house at 5:30 a.m. to write before working all day at my office. My son asked why, if I was going to work early, couldn't I come home early. I didn't sugarcoat it. I explained that this was a busy season and that Mommy had to work additional hours but that in a few more weeks, when the manuscript was finished, I would be around more. Our children learn by example, and if we are always honest with them, they will learn to trust us.

Be a Mom Who Involves Kids in Chores

It is important to involve kids, from a very young age, in household tasks. Doing so helps you feel less stretched too thin because more hands mean less work for you. It also teaches them the value of pitching in and that, to make a house a home, everyone needs to take pride in it. Just because you work does not mean you should feel guilty if some of your time with your kids is spent folding laundry or cleaning windows. Instead, embrace that being their parent means teaching them how to live well—and that includes learning how to clean up.

Be a Mom Who Says Sorry and Accepts Apologies

If you make a mistake, be quick to apologize. Not teaching your children the value of admitting wrongdoing is hurtful to them both immediately and in the future. Your vulnerability, particularly as your children get older, will translate into respect from your children. The act of apologizing also teaches your children the value of owning mistakes and making things right.

Moreover, apologizing is a gift to yourself. In *Why Won't You Apologize? Healing Big Betrayals and Everyday Hurts*, Harriet Lerner writes, "Our self-respect and level of maturity rest squarely on our ability to see ourselves objectively, to take a clear-eyed look at the ways that our behavior affects others, and to acknowledge when we have acted at another person's expense."[13] You might be quick to beat yourself up for overreacting and making a poor choice in your parenting, but when you apologize, you make things right and experience freedom from self-inflicted guilt and shame.

An apology shows that if you act in a hurtful manner, you can repair the relationship. You won't leave things undone and fractured. The ability to see things for what they really are and seek to make things whole is a beautiful gift you can give your children.

Likewise, when your children apologize to you, respond with compassion, gratitude, and grace. Recognize the courage it takes to apologize. Say thank you, and then move on. You may be tempted to use the apology to remind them what they did wrong, but this diminishes the apology and makes the child feel bad.[14] For example, don't say, "Thank you for apologizing. What you did was very wrong and hurtful. Don't do it again." When your child says sorry, it is not the time for additional instruction.

Be a Mom Who Is Present and a Good Listener

The greatest gift you can give your children is to be present and attentive when you are with them. Because I am away from my children for the majority of the day, when I am with them, I try to give them my full attention. Giving your children the gift of your undivided attention shows them that you care.

As your children grow, do less talking and more listening. Don't let work and other responsibilities get in the way of having conversations with your kids. Pay attention not just to the words coming from your children's mouths but also to their body language. As kids mature into teenagers, they sometimes are less open, which is why it is imperative to pay attention to verbal and nonverbal cues. Lean in when they are talking, and respond thoughtfully and gently. One mother, Holly, shared a story about her daughter getting kicked out of a friend group and the critical role listening played in her daughter's healing.

> My husband and I worked hard to find ways to listen, ways to encourage her to talk when she needed it, ways to give her feedback on how she was navigating a very difficult situation, and we gave her ways out if needed. . . . The entire semester proved challenging for her and for us, but checking in with her through a variety of ways—verbal conversations, car conversations, texting, and sending memes—gave us ways to start and continue conversations and opportunities to listen.[15]

This example demonstrates the positive impact you can have on your children when you really listen. Honor the gift of their words, and be slow to interject opinions and criticism.

Be a Mom Who Welcomes Friends

Friends play an important role in your children's lives, particularly as they get older. When I was growing up, everyone hung out at my house. My mom never said no to hosting friends, and that had a profound impact on me, though I couldn't articulate it until I was an adult.

Nicole, an executive and mom of three, shared:

> When my daughter was in high school, she was involved in everything and kids were always at our home. After a long day of work or a week of traveling, sometimes it would get old. That said, I learned how important it was to include her friends in some of our family activities, even something as simple as dinner or an evening at home together. I learned a lot about her friends, her friends' lives, even her friends' relationships with their mothers. It helped my daughter and me become closer by getting to know the people who were important to her and showing her that they were important to me.[16]

This welcoming nature also extends to boyfriends and girlfriends. If your child is in a relationship, be inviting to his or her significant other. Cultivating a healthy, positive relationship is important for everyone. Having an open-door policy for your children's friends will help enrich your relationships and build trust.

Be a Mom Who Says Yes

Have you ever said no to your child and when they asked why, your reply was, "Because I said so"? I know I have. Usually, this response is born out of my exhausted, stretched-too-thin perspective. I don't want to help. I don't want them to drag those toys out.

Me, me, me. These kinds of no's can really impact our kids, their respect for us, and the way they see us. Instead, shift to saying yes often.

I learned a great deal about saying yes more often from Brené Brown in her COURAGEworks course. "Our goal as parents should be to give kids an inspired yes every single time we can," she says. In her course, Brené teaches that saying yes inspires trust with our kids. But remember, it is possible to say yes and put boundaries within that yes. For instance, maybe your child asks if they can go with some friends to a nearby park. Yes, it would be the farthest they have walked before without an adult, but rather than jumping immediately to a no response, maybe say something like, "Yes, but I am going to follow on my bike just to be sure you are safe. I trust that you will be, but let's do this in-between step first." By making your response a yes instead of a "no, you're not ready," you inspire trust and develop the relationship.

This doesn't mean you should say yes to things that are inappropriate for your children. For instance, if your child wants to have a cell phone but is ten years old and you don't feel it is appropriate, you might say, "Yes, you can have a cell phone when you are thirteen." When they balk and complain that you don't trust them, you can reply, "I trust you, but I don't trust some of the things that are accessible from a cell phone." This type of yes shows your child that they have room to grow toward the yes. When you say yes, you empower your children and help them flourish. And sometimes those yeses also turn into memories made together.[17]

Be a Mom Who Sets Boundaries and Follows Through

Brené Brown's COURAGEworks course also reminded me how important it is for our children to learn boundaries because boundaries set expectations for the ways we live and behave. She offered the following insights regarding how to set effective boundaries.

As you set boundaries for your family, be sure to explain them in an accessible way. The why is just as important as the what. Consider your family's values, and remember that the boundaries you set demonstrate the love you have for your children, even though your kids won't always understand that in the moment. Trust that when they are older, your kids will see how your boundaries positively impacted them.

Remember that boundaries can be difficult for children. A boundary might upset them. When this happens, allow your children to express their feelings. Sometimes I'm tempted to make things better for my kids when I set a boundary that upsets them. "You can't do this, but let's do this instead." I hate seeing them upset, but I must remember that learning to feel is an important part of the growing-up journey. It is not my job as a parent to always make my children happy. It is my job to help them grow into healthy adults. Fixing their anger, sadness, or frustration about a boundary is not helpful to me or my kids. As you set boundaries, make space for your children's feelings related to those boundaries, but don't change the boundaries in light of their feelings.[18]

Be a Mom, Not a Martyr

Sometimes working moms are tempted to view motherhood from a martyr's perspective: *There's so much to do, and I have to do it all. I have to sacrifice all my needs for the good of my children. There's no rest for the weary.* I remember going to work when my children were babies and wearing my exhaustion like a badge of honor. I would tout about the little sleep I got and chock it up to the perils of motherhood.

Motherhood is not a calling for martyrdom. Being a parent does not mean you need to give up all your own needs and burn the candle at both ends. You can invest in your family while still loving yourself. So be a mom who loves her kids wildly and can also say, "No, I am not going to worry about XYZ right now (or ever)."

Be a Mom Who Plays

Shonda Rhimes, working mom and critically acclaimed, award-winning creator and executive producer of numerous hit television series, writes in her book *Year of Yes: How to Dance It Out, Stand in the Sun, and Be Your Own Person* about a time she was headed to an event wearing a ball gown when her daughter asked, "Wanna play?" That question was a transformative moment in Shonda's parenting. She said yes and plopped down in her gown to read to her daughter, dance, sing "Head, Shoulders, Knees, and Toes," and get lots of sticky kisses. "Then I got in the car to go to the event," she recalls. "Happy. That warm joy in me. Feeling fundamentally changed. Like I knew a secret that very few people get to learn. But really it was just love. That's no secret. It's just something we forget. We could all use a little more love."[19]

After working all day, you may not feel like playing. But say yes anyway. After reading Shonda's book, I thought about all the times I didn't say yes to play, instead suggesting, "Why don't you play with your brother/sister instead?" I decided to change that—although my playtimes never involve ball gowns and diamonds like Shonda's! I say yes to dressing Barbies and playing pretend with my daughter. I say yes when my son challenges me to a game of chess. I say yes to building block towers with my three-year-old. And you know what? I never, ever regret playing. I never feel like play is a misuse of my time. In fact, I feel like play is the *best* way I can spend it.

So if play sometimes feels like a burden, know you are not alone. But say yes anyway. Try incorporating more play into your day with your kids. As they get older, play might mean game night, watching funny YouTube videos, creating something together, or going outside for a game of hoops. However you play, enjoy the meaningful connection it will foster with your children.

Be a Mom Who Is Real, Not Perfect

Motherhood is not about Pinterest perfect meals and June Cleaver pearls. It is your hardest, best job. Be willing to let your kids see your imperfections and have imperfect experiences. Let your kids see the real you, not just a polished veneer. I let my kids see me cry because I know putting on a happy face won't help them in the long run. Seeing adults work through emotions is good for them.

When you stop trying so hard to be perfect and start embracing the messiness of each day, your kids will grow with a healthy understanding of what real life looks like.

Be a Mom Who Shows Up

Mothering well is about showing up. Your children will know they are loved when you are there for life's big and little moments. You are there when homework is hard and you are sitting beside them at the dining room table. You are there when they are sick, making chicken noodle soup (maybe out of a can, but whatever) and offering purple chewables. You are there for the aftermath of that first big fight with a friend. You are there for the sporting event wins and for the losses.

While work might *limit* your experiences of being present, it doesn't *eliminate* them. Work doesn't lessen your ability to show up when it counts, and mothering is a calling that extends well beyond nine to five. You are a good mom because you are there for your children. They know you are someone they can talk to and depend on—and no job is going to prevent that from happening.

During a busy season in my life, I was texting with a friend whose children are about ten years older than mine. She had posted something online about treasuring the years when they are little that had really connected with me. She said, "You are slaying the little stage. You are going to be so proud of it in fifteen years. You are such a good mom." When I replied that I felt like I was slaying nothing because I was so overwhelmed, she said, "Lies. All lies. Put them in the garbage and shut the lid. You could not parent the next three years, and your kids would still feel cherished beyond all reason. This is a short season."

Her words made me tear up because I knew she was right. I was stretched too thin and allowing myself to believe a lie that I was not parenting well.

Parenting isn't about a single moment or even a single season. It takes place day in and day out as you do one right thing after another. If you are in a season when you feel like you aren't at your best for your kids, do the best you can. Your kids know you love them. Because you do. Wildly and without limit. Work, responsibilities, and the stresses of day-to-day life cannot take that away from them—or you.

Reflections on Your Parenting

What daily and weekly practices are important to you in parenting your children?

_____

_____

_____

_____

As you consider the times of day you have with your children, how can you intentionally focus on them? Use the grid below to document habits you can put into practice. If you are not home with your children during a particular time, simply record N/A.

Morning	
Lunch	
Afternoon	
Evening	
Weekend	

How does your work impact your family—positively and negatively? _____

_____

_____

When you think about your role as a mother, what do you want your children to remember about you? How can you ensure that this is the memory you are giving to them?

What is one habit you can work on in your parenting? Using the SMARTER system, write a goal to help you in this area.

This chapter includes a series of "be a mom who is" statements. Which one resonated with you the most and why?

_____

_____

_____

_____

Do you have a family mission statement? If not, take time to write one as a family. This will help to guide you and your family's priorities.

Gratitude fosters togetherness and happiness within families. Consider buying a piece of poster board and creating a family gratitude board.

EIGHT

Creating a Home You Love

On a girls' trip with some friends, I confessed something to my friend Lisa. "I have a lot of shame about my home. I cannot stay on top of the cleaning and maintenance."

She answered, "You should write about that."

So now I'm telling you.

Keeping house is not my thing. I want it to be. I subscribe to all the magazines: *Southern Living*, *Real Simple*, *Country Living*, and *Better Homes and Gardens*. I've ripped out their pages and pinned their photos on Pinterest. I've thought about my childhood and how my working mom always kept our home neat and tidy. However, I really struggle. There's always more to put away—more kid stuff, more mail, more dishes. And with work, kids, and life, the house gets the short end of the stick.

Time and time again, when people ask me how I do it all, I usually laugh and say, "Trust me, if you saw my house, you would know that I don't do it all—not even close!" Around our house, the laundry is almost never completely put away and the toys always need wrangling. And then there's the dishwasher—why can't it unload itself?

Sound familiar?

According to the Pew Research Center, 31 percent of mothers who work tend to take on more household chores and responsibilities, while 59 percent said they are shared equally by mothers and fathers.[1] But regardless of whether you take on more household chores or you split them equally, household work is a struggle for most working moms. In fact, in my survey of two thousand working moms, four out of five said that home management (including cooking, cleaning, errands, etc.) was something with which they struggle. A few of the comments made regarding the home included these:

The number one thing that stresses me out as a working mom is my house. I completely understand the idea of "spend time with your kids now—the house will always be there," but my house is a pig pen all the time. Because I never have time to clean. My kids are old enough to help, and still it's always a disaster. We *never* have friends over because of it, and if someone unexpectedly knocks on our door, we go outside to talk to them. I hate, hate, hate it.

My house is pretty much always a mess, despite my trying to clean it. It feels so endless, and I also hate coming home and spending the time I finally have to relax with my kiddo and husband cleaning instead. It's a huge stress in life.

Our house is a mess all the time. There just aren't enough hours in the day to get everything else done and maintain the house. I've considered a cleaning lady but never done it.

I struggle to just clean the basic areas and never have time to deep clean or organize anything. I make time with my husband and children a priority, so the tidiness of the house suffers.

My house is always a disaster, and I'm always playing a game of catch up to the loads of laundry, piles of dog poop, and endless questions of "What's for dinner?"

These feelings are not unusual. In fact, according to research by UCLA-affiliated social scientists, "American families are overwhelmed by clutter, too busy to go in their own backyards, rarely eat dinner together even though they claim family meals as a goal, and can't park their cars in the garage because they're crammed with non-vehicular stuff." The same study also stated, "Managing the volume of possessions is such a crushing problem in many homes that it elevates levels of stress hormones for mothers."[2] Though that study took place in California, it resonates with families across the country. Stuff and a lack of time are overwhelming many of us, and they can be particularly debilitating for working moms who spend a large part of the day working. But life doesn't have to be that way.

I've learned that my house is never going to be like the ones in magazines, and instead of feeling shame, I am embracing the truth that my house doesn't have to be perfect for me to feel content in it. I'm also working to incorporate habits, systems, and services to make things easier.

You too can overcome the overwhelm by making choices to improve things in your home. Change won't happen overnight, but by starting small, evaluating ways to incorporate habits and systems in your home, and finding services that can help you fill in the gaps, you can feel more peace at home.

Routines Lead to Habits

Habits are defined as regular practices of any kind. You can possess good habits, bad habits, or habits that are neither good or bad, just processes that you do because you're in a rut or they just feel right. Think about your habits for a moment, specifically those that involve common household chores such as laundry, dishes, vacuuming, paying bills, and the like. Do you have a proactive strategy for your home? Or are you reactive with household chores? Maybe you're both, depending on the task at hand. If you tend to something only when it can't wait any longer, your actions are likely contributing to your feelings of chaos and discontentment.

I could write an entire chapter on feelings of chaos at home, because it is a *big* struggle for our family. One example: We have a craft room above our garage. For nearly a year, I crafted in it very little. (That sentence makes me sad, but that was the season of life I was in.) Instead, the craft room turned into a bit of a dumping ground, the counters covered with school projects that I planned to scan someday, the table a mess of art supplies that needed to be put away properly. I was embarrassed to go in it myself and was thankful two doors blocked guests from seeing it. The kids would have friends over, and I would be sure to remind them that the craft room was off-limits. I finally decided enough was enough.

I blocked off a Saturday afternoon to declutter and tidy up. I needed to get it done so I could get the room painted (we had stripped the wallpaper two years prior!) and make it the room I had always dreamed of. So while the kids were playing, I went up there to start clearing things out. I felt like a boss. This was getting done.

And then I saw it.

Mouse poop.

Yep, apparently a mouse had taken advantage of the quiet and the clutter to make himself a home.

In *my* craft room.

I lost my mind. My husband was out of town, and I texted him frantically, THERE'S A MOUSE IN THE CRAFT ROOM. WELL, THERE'S POOP. THERE IS POOP.

I obviously couldn't clean anymore.

The next day I got traps—probably quadruple what we needed, but I wasn't messing around. That mouse didn't know what he was dealing with when he slipped in through our garage.

Thankfully, the mouse met his end while enjoying a tasty peanut butter treat, and I was able to get back to my cleaning project. But I was reminded of a valuable lesson: our bad habits can make things worse in the long run. In my case, not only did I have a ton of cleaning to do because of my lack of follow-through with putting things away, but I also had to catch a mouse.

Dana K. White, author of *How to Manage Your Home without Losing Your Mind* and founder of the site A Slob Comes Clean, said this in an interview:

> Looking at the "total mess" is overwhelming, so the key to getting started is not to view your home as one big project. That makes it seem like you need to set aside a week to do nothing but clean. But who has a whole week to devote to that? Start small. Small routines done consistently will have a shockingly positive impact on your home, no matter how messy it is. I recommend starting by making your dishes a daily habit, but if you have your dishes under control, choose something else that makes you crazy. Solve that problem today. Then (and this is the key) solve it again to-morrow *before it becomes a problem again*. Do this every day, and after seven days, you'll have found a way to make this a routine that works in your home. Turning frustrations into routines has a bigger impact than I ever imagined.[3]

Following Dana's advice of turning frustrations into routines can help working moms make positive changes in their homes. When we take those new routines and build habits around them, we bring more sanity to our homes. On the other hand, routines and habits that create chaos will lead to more stress.

In Charles Duhigg's book, *The Power of Habit: Why We Do What We Do in Life and Business*, he outlines what blogger James Clear describes as the 3 R's of habit formation:

1. Reminder: the cue or trigger that starts the habit
2. Routine: the action you take, which is the habit itself
3. Reward: the benefit you gain from doing that habit[4]

As you consider what habits you might need to change or begin in your home, reflect on these three R's. For me, I would like to get better at staying on top of the laundry. So a new habit that I am forming is that every morning I fold a load of laundry before work. My R's look like this:

1. Reminder: each morning I turn on the dryer (the buzzer is the reminder to fold it)
2. Routine: fold the laundry
3. Reward: less dirty laundry to tend to

In this chapter's journaling exercise, you'll consider three new routines you can form habits around to help with your home management and stress levels.

On the website Apartment Therapy, writer Shifrah Combiths says that the habit of "completing the cycle" is transformative for a home, and I have to agree. She writes, "Completing the cycle is a synergistic mix of Leaving Things As You Found Them and Not Leaving Things That Can Be Done Now For Later."[5] The people who live under my roof are all terrible at completing the cycle, including me. But we are working on it, and the phrase "completing the cycle" is now a part of our everyday vernacular. This incredibly simple concept has had profound ripple effects in the order and feel of our home.

Organize with Purpose

My husband and I are voracious readers and book lovers. Books arriving in the mail multiple times a week is not unusual. The good news is that we always have something to read; the bad news is that we are constantly fighting clutter. I realized that our current system of stacking books two deep on our bookshelf and taking boxes of books to the used bookstore every few months was not working well enough. I realized that this overflow started happening when we moved into our home and got rid of the bookshelf we used to have in our bedroom. After doing some online shopping, I found the perfect shelf that would coordinate with our bedroom furniture. I then cleaned out the downstairs bookshelf, gathering books to donate and books to put upstairs. I also called a handyman to assemble the shelf and take care of a few other home projects, knowing that having him come would be the fastest solution.

Within a week, the shelf was built, the books were on it, and everything was much less cluttered. This organization brought instant peace to our living room, which had been suffering from the weight of overflowing shelves. It's true that the state of a room can have an impact on the state of a person's mind. That cluttered bookshelf had been the physical representation of everything that was wrong with my stretched too thin life. Creating some organization brought much peace.

Organization is critical for working moms to maintain (or create) order. Doing so frees our minds, gives us more time to be with our families, and saves money (no more buying rubber totes or renting storage units for our junk!).

It's important to recognize that your organization style might not be pretty boxes all in a row. You might like to have your things out in the open so you can see what you have. In fact, Kelly Mc-Menamin, professional organizer and cofounder of PixiesDidIt with her sister Katie, said there are four main "pixie personality types" when it comes to organizing: classics, funs, organics, and smarts. These different personalities approach organization very differently. "Classics and funs are detail-oriented and tidy and organize in similar ways. But classics and funs part ways when it comes to structuring time. Classics like to structure time, and funs prefer to be more flexible with it," said Kelly. She then went on to say, "Organics and smarts are bigger-picture thinkers and organize in similar ways (they're the pilers among us). But some smarts and organics part ways when it comes to structuring time."[6]

Recognizing your "pixie personality" or organization style can help you understand and embrace *you*. For instance, instead of feeling guilt or shame about your piles, recognize that piles might be how you best manage paperwork. Then create systems that will help you stay organized using piles, such as baskets for corralling them.

Change is not going to happen instantly, particularly when you have a lot on your plate. You might not be able to predict how long an organizing project will take, but what you can do is commit to staying on task until you complete the project. By staying focused, even if that means setting aside just fifteen minutes a day to get it done, you will more likely be successful and equipped to move on to that bigger project (hello, garage or storage room!).

If you feel overwhelmed by the thought of getting started with organizing, Jennifer Lifford, author of *The Home Decluttering Diet*, recommends the following:

> Try to find an area of your home that isn't too big and will really make an impact on your lifestyle. For example, if morning routines are always chaotic because your kids can't find their shoes and you're constantly misplacing your car keys, start working on creating an organized entryway, closet, or mudroom where you can keep everything that you need daily in a designated spot. If that is even too overwhelming, just pick a drawer or cupboard to get started with. The key is to just get started![7]

In the following pages, we'll look at some practical strategies for clearing clutter, getting organized, and implementing practical changes in your home.

Declutter

The biggest impact you can make on your home is to get rid of stuff. Most of us simply have way too much. Joshua Becker, in *Clutterfree with Kids*, says, "There is more joy found in owning less than can ever be found in organizing more."[8] Isn't that so true?

Creating a Home You Love

Excess is overwhelming our homes, our minds, and our lives. I started decluttering this year and filled up my van five times with donations packed in garbage bags and boxes. And I swear, I hardly made a dent in our home. But the process motivated me to get rid of even more. I am at the point where I can't stop. Nothing is safe. The more I get rid of, the more I want to get rid of. Every time a big box is delivered to our home with staples such as diapers and paper towels, I fill it up with things to donate. One box in means one box out. I also have a basket in our hallway upstairs for depositing too-small clothes, toys that are no longer played with, and random knickknacks. By having a place to drop the unwanted items, you are more likely to actually get rid of those things.

I have also been very intentional about involving my children in decluttering because it is an opportunity to talk with them about how donating their things will help another child. It also teaches them about avoiding excess and how when we keep only the things we truly enjoy, we are happier.

As you think about clutter in your own home, consider the areas that are spilling over. Are your closets too full? Are baskets of toys overflowing in your kids' room? Start decluttering these areas, and you will find that as things become tidier, you will be more motivated to move to other areas.

Sort by Category

Sorting is a principle promoted by Marie Kondo of *The Life-Changing Magic of Tidying Up* fame. Her philosophy is that you need to gather everything of a particular category together before you can truly organize and purge.[9] I have found this to be true in my home, which is two stories. If I clean only the downstairs' bathroom closet, I am unable to truly know all that I have because the same items may be upstairs too. Take the time to sort by category so that you know what you have too much of, what you need, and what belongs where in your home.

Hang Things Up

Nothing should be on the floor. Invest in hooks and racks for hanging things up. From gardening tools to chairs to jewelry, hooks are your friend. You will be amazed by how much neater your home is when things are hung up. We installed hooks adjacent to the door leading into the garage for pool bags and backpacks that need to be grabbed on the way out the door. Doing so took only thirty minutes but instantly made things feel lighter in our home.

Give Everything a Home

My daughter's room was a constant mess. Barbies, dress-up clothes, stuffed toys. Adeline went from one play endeavor to another with little regard for putting her things away. While I had bins and boxes for her toys, nothing was labeled or assigned in a way that made sense to Adeline. One Sunday afternoon we spent the day in her room boxing up toys to donate and assigning homes for her remaining toys. By giving everything a home, we made it easier for her to keep her room neat.

Use Boxes and Baskets for Wrangling

For many people, storing items in inaccessible ways means those items never get used. Bins and baskets are every busy mother's friend because they make cleanup a snap and keep belongings accessible and visible. The possibilities are endless, and they are usually pretty too.

In our home, we have baskets near our front door for shoes. When my children come home and take off their shoes, the shoes go in the baskets. That simple system keeps our front entryway free of clutter. We created the basket system after recognizing that shoes were always by the door. Recognizing the rhythms of where things get left is a good way to determine where organization tactics can be deployed.

We also use baskets in our closets and cabinets and to gather up large toys. They are pretty and easy to maintain. Plus, they help keep things in order.

Speed Clean

Speed cleaning is a trick my mom taught me that works great for busy parents on the go. Keep cleaning products accessible, and do a little bit of cleaning whenever you are in a room. For instance, if you are in the bathroom, take thirty seconds to put away the things left out on the counter. Wipe down the mirror with a Windex wipe. Do a quick sweep of the toilet bowl.

Professional cleaner Briana Short agrees with my mom and advises that quick daily cleaning habits make a huge difference in a home, especially in kitchens and bathrooms, which are highly trafficked. Her advice for kitchens is this:

> Countertops tend to get dirty very quickly, with crumbs from the toaster, sauces from dinner prep, and all other food prep that goes on. Keep a container of cleaning wipes under the sink and use these once a day to wipe down countertops. This will sanitize the surface and keep debris from building up. Feeling ambitious? Take your cleaning wipe when wiping the countertops and hit the knobs/pulls on your cabinets/drawers. These tend to get super sticky with hands covered in sauces and spices when cooking.[10]

Encourage your family members to follow these quick-cleaning tips to help keep things cleaner. If everyone does ten minutes a day, those bite-sized portions could add up to hours of cleaning each week that don't feel daunting.

Teach Accountability

Teaching accountability can be transformative in keeping a home. Everyone in it needs to be accountable for their things.

Teaching children good habits when they are young and holding them accountable to pick up after themselves and do chores to help maintain the home are critical. As I mentioned in the last chapter, in our home, we have a simple wipe-off chart in the bathroom with daily habits and chores. Our kids are responsible for completing the items each day before they get privileges such as using electronic devices. This accountability is incredibly helpful in our home now and will serve them well throughout their lives.

Do What Works for You

Using these simple tips as a jumping-off point for creating a more organized home will hopefully provide you with the motivation you need. Keeping a home while working and having a family is difficult. But by continually pursuing order and creating organization systems, you will find yourself feeling less overwhelmed.

Consider what systems you could put in place to keep your home more organized and you feeling less stretched too thin. As you implement systems, you might have to do some decluttering and organizing. While this is time-consuming and may be a hassle in the moment, it will be worthwhile in the long run.

Also remember that what you see in magazines or what appears to be pretty may not be the best solution for your home. Professional organizers Joni and Kitt of Practically Perfect LA say:

> Many people love the way a pantry looks when all food items are decanted into jars or containers—but not all individuals have the time and energy to maintain this type of system on a regular basis, as it adds an extra step to the food shopping and organizing process. Likewise, many clients love the idea of storing their shoes in matching boxes. But if these clients also like to try on several pairs of shoes when they are getting dressed, they might find it cumbersome to place every pair back into the boxes each day. It's imperative to think all of these things through before

diving into a project and to think about the process—not just the finished product.[11]

Make choices that will help make things easier at home, not more difficult. Also, if an organization system doesn't work, don't be afraid to change it. It is better to fix it than let it continue to be a challenge and a time suck.

Lastly, if you are really stuck when it comes to organization, bring in a professional. There is no shame in asking for help. Typically, an organization professional will schedule a consultation with you to learn about your problem areas and your family's needs. They will then develop a plan and get to work. Professional organizers work solo or with the client, depending on the client's preference. Sometimes letting the organizer do the work and then making changes is easier. But some people want to be involved every step of the way, and that is okay too.

Explore Helps and Services

In Elizabeth Vargas's book *Between Breaths: A Memoir of Panic and Addiction*, she talks about a therapy session she had at a rehabilitation center during her battle with alcoholism. During this particular exercise, the participants were blindfolded and required to go through a rope maze. If they needed help, they could raise their hands. Elizabeth shared how she kept hearing others finish the maze, but she continued to walk into walls and fumble around. Finally, after hitting what felt like the fifteenth wall and becoming incredibly frustrated, she raised her hand. Someone came to her side and guided her through to the end. Only after she asked for help was she able to finish the maze. In fact, nobody made it through alone. In her story, the center used the exercise as a metaphor that no one can recover from addiction alone.[12] This story hit me deeply because I realized the same thing is true for all areas of life. We are not meant to do things alone. Asking for help is not just okay; it is necessary.

In addition to incorporating positive habits and organizing with purpose, a third way to better manage your home is to sign up for services that can help fill the gaps and give you more time to do the things only you can do. In a 2014 survey by Care.com, one in four moms reported crying once a week due to the stress of "having it all," and 29 percent of the moms said they could afford to hire help but didn't because of feelings of guilt.[13] If you fall into the stressed, crying, and/or feeling guilty camp, let me assure you that you should not feel this way. Asking for help is an important skill in succeeding in managing your home well.

Here are a few of my favorite types of services.

Delivery Services

Thanks to the internet, pretty much everything can be delivered to you. Amazon, Target, Honest Company, and Grove Collaborative are just four of the many companies whose shoppers can schedule the delivery of household products to their homes on a regular basis. I couldn't manage my home without these services. They save me an incredible amount of time and money and have eliminated the need for me to go to a big box store for any household staple.

I also use shopping services such as Stitch Fix, Trunk Club, Gwynnie Bee, thredUP, and Rocksbox to have clothing and accessories sent to me. For instance, when I needed some new black boots for fall, I emailed my stylist at Trunk Club, shared what I was looking for, and within a week, a box with ten pairs of boots arrived. I tried them all on at home, kept a pair, and sent the rest back, paying only for what I kept. This service prevented me from having to go to multiple stores to try on shoes and delivered exactly what I needed. Evaluate the stores you regularly visit and see if you can find online services to eliminate some of those trips and save you time.

Food Delivery

A variety of food delivery services can take the stress out of grocery shopping and meal planning. Blue Apron, Plated, Freshly, and HelloFresh all offer delivery of fresh ingredients and recipes to help you make delicious meals at home. Other businesses such as Schwan's deliver frozen items. Also, an increasing number of local grocery stores, Targets, and Sam's Clubs along with companies such as Shipt and Instacart offer grocery pickup options or delivery for a small fee. I use all of these services, and while sometimes they cost a bit more, the time savings and the freeing up of my headspace make them worth it. I also find that they help me plan out meals in advance and not waste as much food.

Service Providers for Cleaning and Home Repair

For those household tasks that you just can't seem to get to, consider hiring a professional. Our family relies heavily on service professionals to ensure that home maintenance gets taken care of and that it is done right. Our biweekly cleaning service brings me peace, knowing that floors and bathtubs are getting scrubbed, sheets are getting changed, and so on. What they get done in two hours would likely take our family an entire Saturday, and they do it better! It is the best money I spend each month.

If you are concerned about price, check local neighborhood groups, Groupon, and Craigslist to find affordable partners.

Maintain the Right Practices

Once you have established the right habits, organization tools, and services for your family, maintain these practices for optimal living. Doing so will help ensure that you continue to be content at home.

Gayle M. Gruenberg, certified professional organizer in chronic disorganization, agrees with this advice, saying, "Regular, ongoing maintenance is the key to success. Even if life gets crazy and things get a little messy, when life calms down and some time can be devoted to putting things away, it's easy and fast to return to the family's desired level of organization."[14]

Maintenance will vary from daily pickup to periodic tweaks to yearly evaluations of what is and isn't working. Professional organizer Jess Nowell advises that daily cleanup is one of the best ways to maintain a more ordered, less messy home.

> This can be done by a number of items, a designated amount of time, and any other measurement you can come up with. It basically gets the family in the habit of every day making sure items get back to their home. So perhaps each person is responsible to make sure five items get back to their home, or there is a five-minute mad dash to see how much can be done, or each room of the house gets looked at on its own day. Find something that works for your family, and get and stay consistent.[15]

Creating order is an investment of time and resources. Don't squander the good work you have done by not maintaining it.

Create Beauty at Home

When I think about homes I love—in real life, in magazines, and online—what makes me love them is how they make me feel. The beauty isn't found in expensive things or formal living rooms but on gallery walls filled with family photos and inspiring quotes. It's found in colorful flowers on a table or a bowl of fruit on the counter.

Just because we get overwhelmed by our homes doesn't mean we can't also find or make beauty in them. In fact, I believe taking time for creating beauty is as important as organizing. No other home is like yours. Invest the time and energy to make it feel like you and your family. What do you want it to say about you? What are the stories you want to share?

One Saturday afternoon I came home from a six-hour writing marathon. My husband decided to run a few errands, and my eldest was outside playing with neighborhood friends. My two youngest children were playing together, and I had a choice. I could fold laundry, which really needed to be done, or I could create a new gallery wall for our home. Ten 8 x 8 wood prints had just arrived, and I was itching to hang them and create a wall celebrating my husband's travels around the world. It was something I had been thinking about for months, and I finally had all the pieces to do it.

This wasn't a difficult choice. I decided to let the laundry wait and design the gallery wall. I knew that every time I climbed our stairs and saw it in front of me it would make me smile. Moreover, it would make my family smile.

The wall turned out beautifully and was a very fulfilling, satisfying project.

Not all beauty needs to be created though. Beauty is everywhere. It's in the drawer of princess dresses. It's in the pot of mums on your front porch. It's in the way the morning sun streams in a window. You'll find satisfaction and wholeness when you change your perspective to recognize beauty every day in your home.

Embrace Your Hardworking Home

Myquillyn Smith, who is my dear friend, home muse to thousands, and author of the bestselling book *The Nesting Place: It Doesn't Have to Be Perfect to Be Beautiful*, has taught me so much that has shaped my perspective of home. She said this in an interview with me:

> A hardworking home that is serving your family well never looks perfect. Isn't that freeing? We don't compare our everyday selves to our wedding portrait; that was a special day when we had a

team of professionals helping us look our best! We also shouldn't compare our homes with magazine photos—another special day when a team of professionals helped a home look its best. Home is happiest when it's being used.[16]

Don't you love thinking of your house as a "hardworking home"? It shifts your thinking from perfect to useful. Find freedom in knowing that your home is a place where you invest in the people you love most in the world. Home is the place where you laugh and play and eat and make messes, and it is *all* good. When my kids leave the nest, I want them to feel like their home was life-giving, full of laughter, truth, prayer, and love. And that can be done even without a living room that looks as if Martha Stewart designed it.

By creating good habits and systems in your home and using services that can save you time, money, and energy, you will have increased bandwidth to focus on the things that really matter to you as a working mom.

Reflections on Your Home

What three habits can you put into place to make managing your home easier? Write out the three R's for each habit.

Habit: _____

1. Reminder: _____

2. Routine: _____

3. Reward: _____

Habit: _____

  1. Reminder: _____

  2. Routine: _____

  3. Reward: _____

Habit: _____

  1. Reminder: _____

  2. Routine: _____

  3. Reward: _____

What systems can you put in place to help reduce clutter and chaos in your home? If you are unsure, brainstorm concerning your home's problem areas and what might help. _____

_____

_____

_____

_____

_____

Circle the area(s) you could use help in at home.

cleaning
organizing
shopping
meal preparation
home maintenance
child care

Consider the types of services described in this chapter and determine which three could help you manage your life with more ease.

_____

_____

_____

_____

NINE

Cultivating Deep Friendships

On Cinco de Mayo, we invited some old friends, Ally and Blake, over to our house for dinner. We'd become friends through church, but after we started attending different churches, we didn't see them often. Though Ally often crossed my mind, I always felt like something else was more pressing, and I never called her. Because she's a homeschooling mom of four, I figured she was busy too. But finally, I decided enough was enough. I sent Ally a text inviting them over for dinner, and she enthusiastically said yes.

That night over chips, salsa, and taco soup, we talked, laughed, and cried for hours. We vulnerably shared struggles and hurts we had experienced in our church and in other friendships, and we listened to them open up as well. We prayed together and hugged them tight when they left. It was one of the most beautiful nights I experienced all year. I know I'll never forget it because it so clearly represented what friendship is supposed to look like. That night I felt truly known and seen.

Looking back on that night reminds me of the importance of investing in friendship, even when work schedules and other responsibilities make doing so difficult. Instead of fighting for time with friends, we too often put it off and think, *Maybe next week or next month when I'm not so busy*. We don't make friendship a priority, and as weeks turn into months, we find ourselves feeling disconnected and lonely and wondering if sending a text or picking up the phone is even worth doing. We scroll through Facebook and Instagram, letting a screen take the place of meaningful relationship. But social media was not created to replace quality time with people we care about.

My friend Nadia, a Buti Yoga master and mom of three, put it this way: "Social media has created more 'friendships' and 'relationships' than we could ever imagine, yet personal connection is lacking more today than ever before, and we are so isolated as a result. Real, meaningful, and healthy friendships with other women are a necessity that requires time and actual one-on-one connection."

She added, "When you go back to ancient and even biblical times, women came together every day in circles, tents, and congregations. These friendships became tribes in and of themselves that lifted and supported them throughout their lives. Sisterhood is one of the most powerful and important aspects in a woman's life that can transform her present and future."[1]

More than 50 percent of working moms who answered my survey said that they found friendships, church, community endeavors, and social commitments challenging to juggle. I want to focus on friendship in this chapter because I know that maintaining friendships is a struggle most of us experience at some point in our journey as working moms. Just because you work and have a family doesn't mean you shouldn't have friends or make time for social engagements. Yes, your other responsibilities make things a bit more complicated, but having friends you can count on, be vulnerable to, and laugh with is very important. Friendship provides a safe place to be your truest self.

Friendship is also important to model for your children. I want my children to see their mommy loving and being loved by people. Unfortunately, sometimes when it comes to making time for friends, working moms will sacrifice that community because they feel guilty for being away from their children. If this is you, know that your children are better off when you take time to be in community with others. You will come back refreshed, refueled, and able to be more present with them. The same benefits your children experience in their friendships are still true for you as an adult.

Okay, so we know that friendship matters. But what does making time for friendship look like? Let's begin by thinking about where you can cultivate community and where you are likely already spending your time. You may need to adjust the way you view some of these places. For instance, do you think about your workplace as just somewhere you go to work, or is it also a place where you get to spend time with people you like every day? As I walk you through the following ideas, consider your perspective and what your current attitudes are toward the people you encounter in various places.

Friendships at Work

Research has shown that when people have friends at work, they are happier and better employees. For instance, a survey conducted by global employee recognition company O. C. Tanner found that "75 percent of employees who have a best friend at work say they feel they're able to take anything on, compared to 58 percent of those who don't have a best friend at work, [and] 72 percent of employees who have a best friend at work are satisfied with their jobs, compared to 54 percent of those who don't have a best friend at work."[2]

Liking the people you work with matters. Don't just work alongside someone; get to know them. When I interviewed for my job,

I asked what the culture was like because it was important to me that the other employees liked one another.

Try inviting a colleague to lunch, hosting a potluck, or simply making time for conversation. Over the years, my colleagues have become some of my closest friends, knowing my day-to-day joys and struggles. We've celebrated weddings, birthdays, and babies and have dined together on countless occasions.

One of the greatest ways I have found to cultivate friendship at work is by getting together outside of work. Because I love to read, I started an office ladies book club. It rotates to a different house every other month and has provided a great way for us to get to know one another better. When we first started the club, we met after dinner and enjoyed light appetizers or dessert with our book discussions. Over time we realized that gathering right after work was more convenient for everyone, and the club turned into literary dinners. We've done everything from Nashville-famous BBQ to homemade lasagna by candlelight. Each dinner is memorable and fun for its own reasons. And after two years of reading books together, the reading has bled into our office culture. We are constantly talking about books we are reading, sharing copies with one another, and connecting on a personal level. As staff members have left or found other jobs, they have continued to be a part of the book club as a way to stay connected. I never would have imagined that an invitation to read a book together would have resulted in such meaningful experiences with my co-workers. But I'm so glad it has.

My co-workers have also supported me through various health-care needs. From the birth of babies to major surgery, they were the first in line to bring meals, put together gift baskets (chocolate and face masks can do a world of good when you are homebound), and text words of concern and encouragement. I texted my office bestie Courtney when I developed an abscess that needed emergency surgical draining. Likewise, I was on her text list for the birth of her first baby and was one of the first to the hospital when sweet Hank was born. I don't know what I'd do without her.

Whether we work full-time or part-time, our colleagues spend a great deal of time with us. They are the ones who get to know us best (if we let them) and are there for both everyday chitchat and major milestones.

If you are self-employed, consider how you can cultivate community while you work. Perhaps work at a coffee shop one day a week or rent shared office space. If your local community has a Facebook group, perhaps write a post asking if other self-employed people would like to gather together to work. Time with other people will benefit you both personally and professionally.

Some women who are self-employed find that their businesses lend themselves to cultivating friendships. For instance, Hillary Ha has a successful business through Young Living and has experienced many friendships through her work in a variety of ways. Some friends have joined her business, and they interact personally and professionally each week. They attend conferences, have conference calls, meet in person, and interact on Facebook. Others have hosted social gatherings where Hillary has brought her business to them, introducing them to essential oils and enjoying quality time with them.[3]

No matter your job, work is where you spend a lot of time. So considering ways to cultivate community in your work is critical to your success—both professionally and personally. If you aren't already doing so, make an effort to strengthen your relationships with those with whom you work.

Friendships with Other Parents

Your children's school and extracurricular activities can also be a great way to make friends. Though you might feel shy at first, start with the common denominator—your children—and go from there. Soon you will be exchanging numbers and finding excuses to get together.

When my son first started playing on a new soccer team, we didn't know anyone. But over the course of the next few seasons, the parents of other kids on his team became some of our closest friends in Nashville. Soccer was just as fun for the parents as it was for the boys who played on the field.

Nina is a mom of two and a full-time sheriff's department lieutenant who works overnight shifts. Her thirteen-year-old daughter is a competitive gymnast who spends more than fifteen hours a week at the gym. With Nina's demanding job, developing trusted relationships was a must. She shared, "With my hours, I can't do it myself. It's good to know I can trust other families on the team."[4] The parents on the team carpool, take care of one another's kids, and provide support when a parent can't be there. They also are good friends to travel with to competitions and other social events.

Developing friendships with parents of your children's friends allows you to spend time with and support your children while also nurturing relationships that benefit you on both a personal and a practical level.

Friendships with Neighbors

Be neighborly! Get to know the people who live near you. Invite them over for dinner, and talk to them when you see one another. My husband and I realized after four and a half years of living in our neighborhood that we had dined with only one set of neighbors a handful of times. Ours is one of five homes in a small cul-de-sac, so for someone like me who yearns for community and loves to share meals, this felt like a travesty. To remedy the situation, I decided to send out a group text inviting everyone over for a cul-de-sac potluck. The responses were very positive. Everyone was excited about getting together and wondered why we had waited so long to do it.

When the weekend of the potluck arrived, I was looking forward to it but also felt a bit overwhelmed. I had a writing deadline, and entertaining didn't feel like the right way to spend my time. Of course, I was wrong. That evening with our neighbors was unforgettable. We laughed and got to know one another better as we sat and talked for more than two hours. The neighborhood gathering was everything I could have dreamed of. All it took was an invitation and blocking off time on the calendar.

Writer Kristin Schell used a turquoise table to get to know her neighbors. She painted a picnic table turquoise and put it in her front lawn. She then started "Front Yard Fridays," when neighbors were invited to come as they were and spend time together. In a *Good Housekeeping* article, she said, "We all long to connect with each other in meaningful ways. When I grew up, we were front-yard people—out in the neighborhood until called home for dinner. I want that for my family."[5]

Kristin's heart reflects a heart desire we all share—to be friendly and known. Her example prompted our family to move some Adirondack chairs to our front lawn, along with a fire pit. The chairs have become a communal place for neighborhood kids and parents to sit and chat. The lure of the occasional marshmallow roast doesn't hurt either.

When someone new moves into your neighborhood, see it as an opportunity to reach out and take them a small welcome gift. Some cookies or a candle can go a long way. When our neighbors decided to build a new house and move away, we prayed for months that a family would move in that had young kids, particularly a daughter the same age as Adeline. I cried when I found out that the family moving in had two kids, including a daughter just a few months younger than our little girl. The day after they moved in, we walked over with a basket full of yummy smelling cleaning products and kitchen towels. Our girls immediately took to each other, playing for well over an hour. When it was time for Adeline to come in, they hugged good night and Adeline happily proclaimed to me, "I made a friend!"

Their sweet and quick friendship was a reminder to me that friendship doesn't have to be complicated. Over the next few months, we enjoyed long chats in the cul-de-sac with the new family, shared vegetables from our garden, and attended cookouts on each other's decks. None of it was complicated, but those simple practices planted seeds for a rich friendship.

Friendships Based on Common Interests

Great friendships can also be cultivated over common interests or habits. Perhaps you always work out at the same barre studio, and you regularly see another woman in the class. Talk to her! Chances are she could use a friend too. If your schedule allows, volunteer at an organization in your local community. You will likely meet people from outside your common circle, and you'll have the pleasure of making a difference in the community at the same time.

Church is another great place to find community. Whether sitting in a pew on Sunday, volunteering in the children's ministry, or attending a small group, you already have a commonality with people there by attending the same place of worship. Take a risk and get to know someone new. You might end up meeting your new best friend. Years ago, while at a new-to-us church, my husband, Matthew, ran into an old acquaintance from college named Todd. His wife, Angie, and I clicked right away. They invited us over for dinner, and the rest is history. Angie and Todd are our eldest son's godparents, and they are our dearest friends—all thanks to saying hello at church. Matthew has taught me so much about how much better life is when you start up conversations with those around you. We have met so many interesting people just by talking. Church is a natural place for this to happen, but it can happen anywhere.

Brooke, a working mom with three children, volunteers in her church, and she and her husband have met some of their closest friends through their experiences serving teenagers in the congregation. They often schedule dinners outside of church with the families. One of the benefits of bringing their families together is that they are able to commune with friends and still have their children around. It's a win-win!

What interests and habits are you pursuing that might provide opportunities for you to make new friends? Pay attention to the people you see in those places, and strike up a conversation the next time you see them.

Making Time for Friendship

Now that we have identified several opportunities for engaging in community, let's talk practically about how to make it happen. Too often working moms will say, "I just don't have the time." Listen, I get it. Recently, I worked close to sixty hours in one week between my day job and a writing project. So time was in short supply. But guess what? I was still able to spend an hour chatting with five moms at the soccer field and an hour having lunch with a friend. And because I've cultivated friendships at work, the forty hours I spent at my day job were with people I enjoy. I also caught up with an old friend on the phone during my commute home. My week was better as a result, because good friends lift us up during the crazy times.

Cara Vincens, a working mom of six, argues that everyone has time for friendship.

> Fitting time in for friends can be as easy as filling in time that you'd most likely waste on social media. Everyone has an hour or two a week to devote to friends. Plan to meet for coffee while your child is at soccer practice, or have breakfast with another mom on your day off after you drop the kids at school. What about taking an evening craft class together? You can chat while you work on the project. Invite a mom over with her children when they come to play. Being a mom of school-aged children is such a great way to meet new people, but it's important to take some of those friendships a bit further than the school yard.[6]

Like Cara asserts, we all have time for friendship. We simply need to recognize the opportunities for cultivating relationships.

We also need to recognize that friendship isn't always about sitting poolside with drinks. Friendships are imperfect and messy and take work. Embracing the real-life, imperfectness of relationships is an important part of allowing friendships to take root and become a priority in your life.

When it comes to making time for friendship—or simply not being overwhelmed by adding it to your life—consider the following important truths.

You Make Time for What Is Important to You

You make time for things you value. Plain and simple. Don't become comfortable with the status quo. You do have the time.

Each year I schedule one or two girls' trips. These trips with my friends allow us to spend quality time together, talk about work, get away from our kids, and refuel. One of these trips is with a group of writer friends. Our first trip was to Hilton Head, and to say it changed my life would be an understatement. I had no idea how fulfilling it would be to get away from work and home and be with other women for a few days—and the beach location didn't hurt. That trip has become a nonnegotiable for me. I save for it, plan my work and family schedule around it, and look forward to it every year. I love that weekend away, and I always come back with a little pep in my step.

While I know trips away aren't in the cards for everyone, the point is that when something is important to you, you find a way to make it happen. If you could use a girls' trip away—or even just a girls' night out—then schedule it. Friendship is something that should be important to you, so make it a priority.

You Have to Want It

If you are feeling lonely and realize you don't have strong community, do what you can to change that. Get to know a neighbor. Volunteer at church. Talk with your co-workers.

Kirsten is a working mom who recognizes the importance of friendship in her life. A few years ago, she signed up for a six-week Bible study through church and got to know several of the women in the group. They all felt a friendship void in their lives and decided to continue gathering after the Bible study ended. These women have become some of Kirsten's closest friends. Sometimes they go out to dinner; sometimes they go to someone's house. The biggest reason their friendship works is because they all *want* to be together. They don't let anything get in the way of their time together.

This reminds me of a season when following through on a double date with our friends Ben and Melissa took Matthew and me more than a year. A year. Multiple times we had something scheduled, and then for one reason or another, our time together got canceled. Finally, on a whim one day, I texted Melissa because Matthew and I had scheduled a babysitter for a date night. They just happened to be free and joined us for dinner. We had an awesome time, but it never would have happened had we not really wanted to spend that time together.

You Have to Make the Effort

I find that I fight for time with friends. I call and text. I schedule lunches. I make the effort—and the rewards are rich. I don't know that I would still be friends with some people if I didn't make the effort because I tend to be the one who always makes our time together happen. That's okay with me though, because those friends are loyal; they just aren't proactive.

Unfortunately, sometimes a friendship is going to feel so one-sided that you'll rightly question if it's worth pursuing. I have had my fair share of friends who were in my life for only a certain period of time. Sometimes they moved away, and we naturally were less close, but other times I was making all the effort and the relationship was clearly not mutually needed. Those realizations are hard, but they are a part of life. Sometimes, though, you will need to be the one who makes the extra effort.

Elizabeth is a design consultant with a thriving but demanding business. She and another woman were neighbors who became good friends. Unfortunately, the friend moved away, and Elizabeth struggled to make time to connect with her. The friend also wasn't putting a lot of effort into the relationship. (This has happened to all of us, hasn't it?) Then Elizabeth received the call that no one wants to get—her friend had cancer. Suddenly, her priorities shifted, and she made time for her friend. Elizabeth called her, went out to lunch with her, and visited her when she wasn't well. During that season, Elizabeth recognized how important it is to make the effort to invest in other people's lives. She recounted, "Just stopping and listening to her has been good for me. It sounds silly and petty when I say it out loud, but it is a change for me and something that I am really trying to work hard on. I don't want it to take something like cancer for me to stop and pay attention to another friend."[7]

You Have to Put It on Your Calendar

Over the years, I have found that I must schedule time for friends on my calendar just as I schedule work meetings and doctor appointments. Meals are a surefire way for me to make time for community. Much of my time spent with friends happens over coffee before work and during hour-long lunch breaks. While your schedule may be different from mine, I'll bet you, too, eat every day. Could you turn one or two of those meals into a time for community?

You Have to Be Okay with Imperfection

Many women today are so afraid to show their imperfections that they let those insecurities get in the way of cultivating friendship. Be okay with being imperfect. Working mom Cathy shared her experience with this, saying, "People don't want to be vulnerable. People don't want to have you over unless their house is perfect or if they don't have makeup on. My neighbor is one of those people. She said, 'I am not the type of person you can just drop in on.' I said, 'Well, I am the type,' and I know she really appreciates that. She feels totally comfortable coming into my home whenever, and I love that."[8] Cathy's openness has shown her time and again the value of being brave enough to say, "My life is not perfect. I am not perfect. But you are welcome." Those words have had a positive impact on numerous relationships in her life. We can all learn from Cathy's willingness to embrace imperfection. When we say yes to opening our doors and letting others into our lives, we can grow friendships that will flourish for years to come.

The Impact of Friendship

With so many other things on our plates every day, why go to so much effort to cultivate friendship? The impact of friendship is vast. The following insights reveal all the powerful ways friendship makes a difference and why it is worth the investment.

Friends Make Us Brave

Last summer I went to Cancun with a group of fifteen girlfriends. We are all writers, and this was a chance for us to take a break from deadlines and family responsibilities and to be together and refuel. We spent a lot of time sitting on the beach, listening to the crash of the waves and to what was on one another's hearts. While sitting there, we often saw people parasailing, their yellow sails high over the beautiful blue water.

Generally speaking, I am not an adventurous person. But something about the serenity of the location and its picturesque beauty made me want to experience it from the air. So I asked if anyone would want to go parasailing with me. At first, just one friend, Jennifer, said, "Yes, I'll totally do it." After two days of talking about it, another friend, Lisa, proclaimed, "I want to go too." That afternoon the three of us plunked down $65 each and made our way to a white taxi boat that would take us deeper into the Gulf of Mexico to our parasailing boat.

As the boat zoomed across the water, I felt the pit in my stomach growing. You know the feeling. Like when you're on a roller coaster and it is slowly making its ascent to the top of the hill. Only we weren't even in the air yet. My friends asked how I was doing, and when I replied that I was nervous, they assured me with big smiles and hand squeezes that it was going to be amazing.

Once we were on the boat, the crew got us into our harnesses, which they clipped to a bar. Our clips also connected us to one another. We were in it together, and there was no going back.

The man helping us, Benito, looked into my eyes and said, "Don't be scared. Smile. Loosen your hands. It's going to be okay." I nodded, took a deep breath, and fake smiled for the camera. The rope started to extend, and we started going up.

My heart beat fast as we went higher and higher in the air. The entire time Lisa and Jen never stopped asking how I was doing. Eventually, the breeze, the view, and their words made me brave. My heart rate slowed. My hands and legs relaxed. We had the most spectacular view of the water, so blue it looked as if it was out of a Pixar movie. We saw a giant sea turtle swimming amid the seaweed. It was one of the most incredible moments of my life. And without my friends, I never would have been brave enough to experience it.

Friends lift us up when we aren't sure we can do something on our own. They make us brave.

Friends Give Us a Safe Space to Process

Sometimes we need to talk things out, and friends are often the sounding boards we need to do that processing. They offer a safe place for us to sort through challenges, bring our worries, share our most vulnerable thoughts, and be our truest selves. There have been many moments in my life when the act of talking through something with a friend gave me the wisdom I needed to make the right choice. Likewise, I have been a safe place for friends who needed me to lend an ear. Oftentimes this sharing isn't about finding an answer but about having someone with us as we journey toward an answer.

Friends Cry with Us

In 2008, my friend Angie and I were pregnant at the same time. (Yes, the same Angie we met at church earlier in this chapter.) She was due in May, and I was due in July. We immediately made plans for our kids to be the best of friends. We imagined how life was going to change with both of us having new babies—Angie's fourth and my first. What we did not imagine was Angie's baby daughter, Audrey, being diagnosed with a condition that would, as the doctors put it, make her incompatible with life. Angie and I cried together a lot those next few months.

I'll never forget when Audrey was born on April 8, 2008. She lived just over two hours. I was able to be at the hospital shortly after Audrey passed away, and I'll never forget what it was like to hold Audrey's tiny body, with my son kicking away in my stomach. Experiencing the beauty and the pain of her short life on that day was terribly difficult. In the days and weeks to come, I wept many times with and for my friend, for her pain was mine too.

Friendship knits us together in deeply profound ways. Those we become closest to suffer when we suffer. It is a gift not to experience those moments alone.

Friends Support Us and Step In When We Need Them

I can think of countless times when friends stepped in to provide support in my life, from watching my kids when I went to the hospital to deliver my son to picking up an extra gallon of milk at the grocery store so I didn't have to run out in bad weather. When my husband went out of town for a month, I was nervous about managing my work responsibilities and parenting duties well. Thanks to my friends, I had no reason to be concerned. They jumped in, texting to check on me, offering to watch my kids, even coming over to help fold a load or two of laundry. I thought that month would be incredibly difficult, but my friends ensured that didn't happen.

When booking summer camps for my kids, I text friends who I know will be willing to carpool, making both of our lives easier. Our neighbors have become dear friends, and I know I can go to them at any time for help.

When my uncle was in hospice, my aunt found great support from friends in her community who sat with her, brought her meals, ran errands for her, and provided shoulders to cry on during the difficult weeks. After he passed away, my aunt shared with me that you really see what a kind friend someone is after you go through the death of a loved one.

The *New York Times* cited a 2006 study of three thousand nurses with breast cancer, highlighting that "women without close friends were four times as likely to die from the disease as women with 10 or more friends. And notably, proximity and the amount of contact with a friend wasn't associated with survival. Just having friends was protective."[9] Isn't that amazing?

In today's fast-paced world, having friends who are willing to step in and provide support can make a huge difference, especially when you are a working parent.

I believe that many working moms miss out on friendship because it is something they don't fight for. Instead, television and social media replace quality time with people. Or busyness and parenting become excuses for why they don't have many friends. If this is you, please don't miss out on friendship. Having a family and a career doesn't mean you can't also have a community of people around you.

If friendship is something you haven't prioritized in a while, I encourage you to do something today that is communally minded.

Maybe you can call or text a friend to check in and let her know she matters to you. A message doesn't have to be long to be meaningful. Reaching out will make a difference both to you and to her.

I hope this chapter causes you to take a look at how you view friendship and community in your own life. You matter, and the people in your life matter. Investing in people is never a waste. Thriving as a working mom involves cultivating rich friendships and making time for community that supports you and is there when you need it.

Reflections on Your Friendships

What kind of community do you enjoy most? One-on-one relationships? Small groups? Events? _____

_____

_____

_____

What do you like about this kind of community? _____

_____

_____

_____

What are the top three qualities you look for in a friend?

1. _____

2. _____

3. _____

Circle the biggest hurdles for you in making time for friends.

Hurdle	Way to Overcome
I don't know anyone.	
I don't have time.	
They don't ever call/text me.	
Their schedules are different from mine.	
I don't have the financial resources to go out.	
We don't live near each other.	
We are not in the same stage of life.	

Look at the hurdles you circled. For each one, identify a way to overcome that hurdle.

What are some ways you can reach out to friends to let them know you care? _____

_____

_____

_____

_____

Take time to plan a lunch with a friend in the coming week. Write down the day and location. _____

_____

_____

_____

TEN

Living a Life You Love

Recently, I listened to the audiobook of Joe Biden's *Promise Me, Dad*, in which he tells of losing his son to cancer. I don't think I have ever cried more while reading a book. I was so moved by the way the Biden family loved one another and served their son and brother while he was sick.

One of the things that struck me most was that Joe Biden was the vice president of the United States at the time, and his work didn't prevent him from being an amazing dad. He did his job as vice president well, overseeing international relations efforts, attending events, and so on, and he still was there for his son in his time of need. Moreover, his son was proud of him. He encouraged Joe in his work. As a working parent, I really connected with Joe's discussion of managing work responsibilities and being actively involved in his son's cancer care. No matter what important situation was happening at work, his family came first.

His story made me remember an analogy I read in the survey I conducted. A mother shared this:

> The best advice I was ever given was to imagine that my life was a juggling act. Some of my balls are glass, and some are rubber. I can

drop the rubber balls and pick them up later, and they aren't any different. However, if I drop a glass ball, it is broken forever—no matter how hard I try to fix it. The key then is to determine which balls are the glass balls.

And so, as we wrap up this book, I wonder, What are your glass balls? What are the things in your life that, if they shattered, would devastate you?

When you look at life through this lens, the answers are easy to see. I think most mothers would say that family is the most fragile and valuable glass ball. That is the ball we don't want to get so much as a hairline crack. If we juggle life's responsibilities, paying the most attention to that precious ball, we will be okay.

As I think about the other balls we've discussed—work, self, home, marriage, friends—I think the answers become more varied for people.

In my life, people, including me, are glass balls. I know that I have to take care of myself so that I can be there for my loved ones. My own glass ball cannot crack. And I certainly don't want to drop the balls that represent my marriage and my friendships. Dropping those balls would be devastating.

But my house? Total rubber ball. My work? Though I sometimes treat it like a glass ball, it is made of rubber. A colleague once said to me, "We are all replaceable," and she was right. I have learned to hold my job loosely, knowing that as much as I love it and take pride in it, my work does not define me.

In her song "Legacy," Nicole Nordeman says it is nice when people say nice things about her but "in the end I'd like to hang my hat on more besides the temporary trappings of this world."

I like how she acknowledges that kind words and recognition can be nice, but at the end of the day, these are not the things that matter. Thriving as a working mother is about finding a rhythm for your life that deepens your relationships and enables you to feel fulfilled. For some working moms, this means making practical changes such as creating more organization in the home. For others, it might mean creating boundaries for work.

Motherhood is the hardest job any of us will ever have. When we layer a career on top of the calling of motherhood, things can be challenging at times—as we have discussed throughout this book! Embracing the following truths can ensure that you are thriving:

- *Everything is a season.* Living life with this outlook has truly transformed my life. If you see life as a series of seasons, it is less likely that you will get overwhelmed. For instance, if my work goes through a busy season and I am working longer hours because of a big deadline, I remind myself that the project has an end date and that my regular hours will resume before too long.

- *Your work is a blessing, not a burden, to your family.* I have been known to apologize to my family for working. One morning my husband called me out, saying, "Stop apologizing. You are good at your work, and our family is fortunate that you have a job." He was right. Having a job that helps support your family is a good thing. Don't lose sight of the good your work brings to your life, even on the days when you just want to stay home.

- *Pinterest perfect is not real life.* Whether it is your home, your food, or your wardrobe, you cannot use social media as a benchmark for what your life should look like. Real life is imperfect. The sooner you stop measuring yourself and the way you live life against impossible standards, the happier you will be. Order that pizza! Don't worry about cleaning up the toys one night! Whatever that thing is that trips up your perspective—let it go. Do you.

- *Your most important relationship is with your husband.* Someday your kids will be gone. You know who won't be gone? Your spouse. Investing in your marriage relationship is so important. Don't neglect one another. If you feel like you are two ships passing in the night, fight to change things. Schedule a date night. Write a love note. Be affectionate.

- *You are a great mom.* Say it loud and proud. Your children were meant for you—not anyone else—to mother them, guide them, teach them, know them. You, just as you are. The fact that you work doesn't diminish the quality of your mothering. Trusting that I am the mother my children need and loving them with reckless abandon have brought such freedom to my life. My work, my emotions, my quirks—all the things that make me me—also make me the mom they need.

As we wrap up this book, let me leave you with this: some days you will feel stretched too thin, and that's okay. It is a part of a life with many responsibilities. You have a lot to juggle. But the goal is for that feeling to no longer be your norm. A life of thriving as a working mom is rich in relationships and happiness. It manifests itself in kisses from loved ones, goals achieved, and contentment. You can live better. So fight for it. Live boldly and passionately. Pursue your dreams, and love your family well.

While our circumstances are different, the one thing that is the same is that we crave to live full, beautiful lives. My hope is that this book has equipped you with ideas and solutions to make your life a little better. I also pray you have seen the beauty in your everyday life and that each day you'll breathe deeply and confidently, knowing that you've got this.

Because you do have it. Your family is so lucky to have you. You are gifted in the work you do each day. You are bright, kind, and passionate. So go forth knowing that, believing that, and living that out. You are a light, and you have the opportunity to shine bright every day in all your different roles. So do that, sister. Thrive and live well.

Reflections on Your Life

When you think about your current life as a working mom, what brings you satisfaction?

_____

_____

_____

_____

What three things do you love about your life?

1. _____

2. _____

3. _____

What does thriving as a working mom mean to you?

_____

_____

_____

_____

What three changes would you like to make in your day-to-day life as you move toward living better and loving your life?

_____

_____

_____

_____

Acknowledgments

To Matthew: None of this would have been possible without you. Your tireless investment into our family, belief in me, and constant support have carried me through the most stretched too thin times. You have my heart and are my safest place. I'll love you all the days of my life.

To Elias: Your hunger for knowledge inspires me to want to learn more with you. Thank you for your bright smile and easygoing attitude. I'm so proud to be your mommy.

To Adeline: Right now, you're six years old, and I already believe you are going to be a woman who changes the world. Never stop fighting for injustice and speaking your truth. Your passion will take you anywhere. Thank you for your love.

To Ezra: You are the best decision our family ever made. Thank you for your endless snuggles and kisses. They are always the best part of a long day.

To my parents, Rick and Debbie: Thank you for teaching me the value of hard work and encouraging me to try new things. I still marvel at how you managed to juggle work and all my extracurriculars as a teenager. I love you both.

To my sister, Melissa: Thank you for your daily phone calls and always keeping it real. I love you. Sissies forever.

To my Aunt Sandy: I cherish our relationship. Thank you for always being there to listen, share your wisdom, and give a good book recommendation.

To the Stretched Too Thin course community: You are the reason this book exists. Your belief in the online course encouraged me to be brave and ask my publisher if I could turn it into a book. Your honest answers to every question I posed over email and Facebook made this a better resource. You are incredible professionals, wives, mothers, and friends.

To the Mom Creative community: Your faithfulness in this journey is one of the most humbling gifts in my life. Thank you for taking the time to read my words, send me messages, and be so loyal. I am deeply grateful.

To my dear friends: I am immeasurably blessed in the friendship department. Much gratitude to the many women who have been so supportive in this journey, especially Angie Smith, Ann Voskamp, Courtney O'Daniel, Jen Hatmaker, Leila Larson, Lisa-Jo Baker, Lindsay Moreno, and Myquillyn Smith. I wouldn't want to do life without you. Also, to one of my oldest friends, Rachel Salsedo: Your thoughtful wisdom and suggested edits made this a much better book.

To our soccer friends, Tim and Shireen Williams, Jeff and Courtney Williams, and Mark Bailey: your friendship to our family is one of our greatest gifts. Thank you for the way you love us and our kids.

To my blogging friends, especially the Girlie Girls tribe and the (in)courage writing team: You are a smart, savvy, strong group of women. Blogging has changed my life in so many ways, but mostly because of women like you.

To my team at Vanderbilt: Thank you to each of you who have celebrated this project, shared opinions on everything from subtitles to book design, and been so supportive. A special shout-out to our book club group too. I am so lucky to call you my colleagues and my friends.

To the Revell team, especially Jen, Abby, Brianna, and Mark: Your collaborative and driven work ethic inspires me to be better. Thank you for your commitment to this message and willingness to embrace my vision. I couldn't ask for a better publishing partner.

To the Choice team: Thank you for believing in me and this book. I will always be grateful.

To Jenni Burke: It's rare to find an agent that you also call a friend. So happy to have found both in you. Thanks for being there for the highs and the lows. Let's go to Italy someday!

To you: Thank you for reading this book. I hope it leaves you inspired. Keep pursuing your passions and loving your family well. The love we show others has a ripple effect that truly impacts the world—and it starts at home.

Appendix

Weekly Time Tracker

Time Tracking: Days 1–4

Time	Day 1	Day 2	Day 3	Day 4
5:00 a.m.				
5:30				
6:00				
6:30				
7:00				
7:30				
8:00				
8:30				
9:00				
9:30				
10:00				
10:30				
11:00				
11:30				
12:00 p.m.				
12:30				
1:00				
1:30				
2:00				

Time Tracking: Days 1–4 (Continued)

Time	Day 1	Day 2	Day 3	Day 4
2:30				
3:00				
3:30				
4:00				
4:30				
5:00				
5:30				
6:00				
6:30				
7:00				
7:30				
8:00				
8:30				
9:00				
9:30				
10:00				
10:30				
11:00				
11:30				

Time Tracking: Days 5–7

Time	Day 5	Day 6	Day 7
5:00 a.m.			
5:30			
6:00			
6:30			
7:00			
7:30			
8:00			
8:30			
9:00			
9:30			
10:00			
10:30			
11:00			
11:30			
12:00 p.m.			
12:30			
1:00			
1:30			
2:00			

Time Tracking: Days 5–7 (Continued)

Time	Day 5	Day 6	Day 7
2:30			
3:00			
3:30			
4:00			
4:30			
5:00			
5:30			
6:00			
6:30			
7:00			
7:30			
8:00			
8:30			
9:00			
9:30			
10:00			
10:30			
11:00			
11:30			

Notes

Introduction

1. Email interview, July 2017.

Chapter 1 Evaluating Your Present

1. The Stretched Too Thin survey, which was conducted in July 2016, included approximately 2,000 working mothers in the United States with children under the age of 18. Respondents answered as follows:

When asked "Do you work?" 68.3 percent said they work outside the home, 9.94 percent said they work at home, and 21.67 percent said they work a combination of both.

When asked "How many hours a week do you work?" 42.05 percent said they work 41 or more hours per week, 36.94 percent said they work 31–40 hours per week, 12.51 percent said they work 21–30 hours per week, and 7.44 percent said they work 10–20 hours per week

When asked "What areas do you find particularly challenging to juggle as a working mom?" 79.9 percent said home management (cleaning, cooking, etc.), 78.05 percent said self-care (hobbies, exercise, health), 65.65 percent said marriage/making time for spouse or significant other, 54.7 percent said friendships, church/community participation, social engagement, 35.55 percent said family commitments, and 35.05 percent said leaving work at work.

2. Phone interview, August 2017.

3. Phone interview, August 2017.

4. Sara Frankl, "Be Thankful—and Don't Miss It," (in)courage, November 8, 2014, http://www.incourage.me/2014/11/be-thankful-and-dont-miss-it.html.

Chapter 2 Setting Yourself Up for Success

1. "2017 Goal Setting, Part 4: Uncover Intentional Goals," Lara Casey: Cultivate What Matters, December 29, 2017, http://laracasey.com/2016/12/29/2017-goal -setting-intentional-goals/.

2. Michael Hyatt, *Your Best Year Ever: A 5-Step Plan for Achieving Your Most Important Goals* (Grand Rapids: Baker Books, 2018), 107–18.

3. To learn more about Laura's time-tracking techniques, check out her book *168 Hours: You Have More Time than You Think* (New York: Portfolio, 2010).

Chapter 3 Discovering the Feelings Within

1. Phone interview, August 2017.

2. Bill Farrel and Pam Farrel, "Understand How a Woman's Brain Is Like Spaghetti," Focus on the Family, accessed March 8, 2018, https://www.focusonthe family.com/marriage/gods-design-for-marriage/why-are-men-like-waffles-why -are-women-like-spaghetti/understand-how-a-womans-brain-is-like-spaghetti.

3. Phone interview, August 2017.

4. Phone interview, August 2017.

5. Phone interview, August 2017.

6. Phone interview, August 2017.

7. Jen Hatmaker, *Of Mess and Moxie: Wrangling Delight Out of This Wild and Glorious Life* (Nashville: Thomas Nelson, 2017), 194.

8. Email interview, September 2017.

9. Email interview, September 2017.

10. Email interview, September 2017.

11. Phone interview, August 2017.

12. Marcus Buckingham, *Find Your Strongest Life: What the Happiest and Most Successful Women Do Differently* (Nashville: Thomas Nelson, 2009), 55.

Chapter 4 Practicing Self-Care

1. Phone interview, August 2017.

2. Email interview, September 2017.

3. Email interview, September 2017.

4. Email interview, January 2018.

5. Email interview, January 2018.

6. Email interview, January 2018.

7. Email interview, January 2018.

8. Email interview, January 2018.

9. Email interview, January 2017.

10. Email interview, January 2018.

11. "Current Physical Activity Guidelines," Centers for Disease Control and Prevention, last updated November 29, 2016, https://www.cdc.gov/cancer/dcpc /prevention/policies_practices/physical_activity/guidelines.htm.

12. Email interview, August 2017.

13. Email interview, September 2017.

14. Email interview, September 2017.

15. Phone interview, August 2017.

16. "Organized Kitchen Drawers and Fridge," *Sunny Side Up*, April 15, 2014, https://www.thesunnysideupblog.com/2014/04/organized-kitchen-drawers-and -fridge/.

17. "How Much Sleep Do We Really Need," National Sleep Foundation, accessed March 8, 2018, https://sleepfoundation.org/excessivesleepiness/content /how-much-sleep-do-we-really-need-0.

18. Brené Brown, *The Gifts of Imperfection: Let Go of Who You Think You're Supposed to Be and Embrace Who You Are* (Center City, MN: Hazeldon Publishing, 2010), 69.

19. Phone interview, August 2017.

20. Adapted from "Getting Started with Mindfulness," Mindful, accessed March 8, 2018, https://www.mindful.org/meditation/mindfulness-getting-started/.

Chapter 5 Finding Rhythm at Work

1. Katharine Brooks, "Job, Career, Calling: Key to Happiness and Meaning at Work?" *Psychology Today*, June 29, 2012, https://www.psychologytoday.com/blog /career-transitions/201206/job-career-calling-key-happiness-and-meaning-work.

2. Sarah Jane Glynn, "Breadwinning Mothers Are Increasingly the U.S. Norm," Center for American Progress, December 19, 2016, https://www.americanprogress .org/issues/women/reports/2016/12/19/295203/breadwinning-mothers-are -increasingly-the-u-s-norm/.

3. Facebook interview, August 2017.

4. Carmen Nobel, "Children Benefit from Having a Working Mom," Harvard Business School, May 15, 2015, https://www.hbs.edu/news/articles/Pages/mcg inn-working-mom.aspx.

5. Facebook interview, August 2017.

6. Phone interview, August 2017.

7. Melissa Dahl, "If You Can't Have the Job You Love, Love the Job You Have," The Cut, April 11, 2016, https://www.thecut.com/2016/04/if-you-cant-have-the -job-you-love-love-the-job-you-have.html.

8. Quentin Forttrell, "The Sad Reason Half of Americans Don't Take All Their Paid Vacation," MarketWatch, May 28, 2017, https://www.marketwatch.com/story /55-of-american-workers-dont-take-all-their-paid-vacation-2016-06-15.

9. Email interview, August 2017.

10. Email interview, August 2017.

11. Susan Sorenson, "Don't Pamper Employees—Engage Them," Gallup, July 2, 2013, http://news.gallup.com/businessjournal/163316/don-pamper-employees-engage.aspx.

12. Email interview, January 2018.

13. Laura Vanderkam, *I Know How She Does It: How Successful Women Make the Most of Their Time* (New York: Portfolio, 2015), 244–47.

14. Steven Rosenfeld, "70 Percent of Americans 'Emotionally Disconnected' at Work: Shocking Poll Reveals Workforce Zombieland," Alternet, June 18, 2013, https://www.alternet.org/corporate-accountability-and-workplace/70-percent-americans-are-emotionally-disconnected-work.

Chapter 6 Investing in Your Marriage

1. "Many Kinds of Intimacy," accessed March 8, 2018, http://www.ldysinger.com/THM_544_Marriage/09b_Hom_Controv/10_12-types-intimacy.htm.

2. Phone interview, August 2017.

3. "Employment Characteristics of Families—2015," Bureau of Labor Statistics, April 22, 2016, https://www.bls.gov/news.release/archives/famee_04222016.pdf.

4. Facebook interview, August 2017.

5. Personal interview, July 2017.

6. Phone interview, August 2017.

7. Phone interview, August 2017.

8. Personal interview, July 2017.

9. Phone interview, August 2017.

Chapter 7 Parenting Well

1. Renee Peterson Trudeau, *Nurturing the Soul of Your Family: 10 Ways to Reconnect and Find Peace in Everyday Life* (Novato, CA: New World Library, 2013), xxii.

2. Email interview, January 2018.

3. Email interview, September 2017.

4. Email interview, September 2017.

5. Personal interview, August 2017.

6. Email interview, January 2018.

7. Email interview, January 2018.

8. Email interview, January 2018.

9. Facebook interview, August 2017.

10. Phone interview, August 2017.

11. Phone interview, August 2017.

12. Email interview, January 2018.

13. Harriet Lerner, PhD, *Why Won't You Apologize? Healing Big Betrayals and Everyday Hurts* (New York: Simon & Schuster, 2017), 175–76.

14. Lerner, *Why Won't You Apologize?*, 97.

15. Email interview, January 2018.

16. Email interview, January 2018.

17. Adapted from Brené Brown, "The Gifts of Imperfect Parenting: A Whole-hearted Revolution" e-course, Boundaries Session, offered 2017.

18. Brown, "The Gifts of Imperfect Parenting."

19. Shonda Rhimes, *Year of Yes: How to Dance It Out, Stand in the Sun, and Be Your Own Person* (New York: Simon & Schuster, 2015), 119.

Chapter 8 Creating a Home You Love

1. "Raising Kids and Running a Household: How Working Parents Share the Load," Pew Research Center, November 4, 2015, http://www.pewsocialtrends.org/2015/11/04/raising-kids-and-running-a-household-how-working-parents-share-the-load/.

2. Beth Teitell, "Today's Families Are Prisoners of Their Own Clutter," *Boston Globe*, July 9, 2012, https://www.bostonglobe.com/lifestyle/2012/07/09/new-study-says-american-families-are-overwhelmed-clutter-rarely-eat-together-and-are-generally-stressed-out-about-all/G4VdOwzXNinxkMhKA1YtyO/story.html.

3. Email interview, September 2017.

4. James Clear, "The 3 R's of Habit Change: How to Start New Habits That Actually Stick," James Clear website, accessed March 8, 2018, https://jamesclear.com/three-steps-habit-change, based on Charles Duhigg, *The Power of Habit: Why We Do What We Do in Life and Business* (New York: Random House, 2012).

5. Shifrah Combiths, "Try the 'Complete the Cycle' Cleaning Method for Instant Results," Apartment Therapy, July 23, 2017, https://www.apartmenttherapy.com/try-complete-the-cycle-and-see-how-much-less-you-have-to-pick-up-221322.

6. Email interview, September 2017.

7. Email interview, September 2017.

8. "Joshua Becker Quotes," Goodreads, accessed March 8, 2018, https://www.goodreads.com/author/quotes/4397208.Joshua_Becker.

9. For more insight into Marie's philosophy, read *The Life-Changing Magic of Tidying Up: The Japanese Art of Decluttering and Organizing* (Berkeley, CA: Ten Speed Press, 2014).

10. Email interview, September 2017.

11. Email interview, September 2017.

12. Elizabeth Vargas, *Between Breaths: A Memoir of Panic and Addiction* (New York: Grand Central Publishing, 2016), 206–207.

13. "Care.com Survey Finds One in Four Working Moms Cry Alone at Least Once a Week," Care.com, October 23, 2014, https://www.care.com/press-release-carecom-finds-1-in-4-moms-cry-alone-once-a-week-p1186-q49877680.html.

14. Phone interview, September 2017.

15. Email interview, September 2017.

16. Email interview, September 2017.

Chapter 9 Cultivating Deep Friendships

1. Email interview, August 2017.

2. Ilan Mochari, "One Surprising Way to Boost Workplace Productivity," Inc.500, April 18, 2016, https://www.inc.com/ilan-mochari/best-friend-at-work-oc-tanner-survey.html.

3. Phone interview, July 2017.

4. Phone interview, July 2017.

5. Christine Kopaczewski, "Front-Yard Friends," *Good Housekeeping*, June 2017, 59–60.

6. Email interview, August 2017.

7. Phone interview, July 2017.

8. Phone interview, July 2017.

9. Tara Parker-Pope, "What Are Friends For? A Longer Life," *New York Times*, April 20, 2009, http://www.nytimes.com/2009/04/21/health/21well.html?_r=0.

Jessica N. Turner is the author of *Stretched Too Thin* and *The Fringe Hours*. She is also an award-winning marketing executive and the founder of the popular lifestyle blog *The Mom Creative* (www.themomcreative.com). An award-winning marketing professional and speaker, Turner has been featured in numerous media outlets, including *The Today Show, O Magazine, Hallmark Home and Family, Pregnancy & Newborn Magazine, Better Homes and Gardens,* and *Inc.com*. She and her family live in Nashville, Tennessee.

For inspiring content about motherhood,
DIY projects, frugal living, product reviews,
and more, visit Jessica's lifestyle blog

TheMomCreative.com

Also connect with her via social media:

🐦 JessicaNTurner	📘 TheMomCreative
📌 JessicaNTurner	▶️ TheMomCreative
📷 JessicaNTurner	📷 BookSnobbery